MEMOIRS

OF THE

REVOLUTION

IN

BENGAL

MEMOIRS

OF THE

REVOLUTION

IN

BENGAL,

ANNO. DOM. 1757

BY

JOHN CAMPBELL ,WILLIAM WATTS

GYAN

Published by

GYAN

Gyan Publishing House
5, Ansari Road
Daryaganj, New Delhi-110002
Phone: 011-47034999, 9811692060
E-mail: books@gyanbooks.com

Distribution Network
gyanbooks.com
India, USA, Canada, UK, Australia

ISBN: 978-93-6280-402-0 (HB)
First Published, 1760

2nd Impression 2024

Printed at: Gyan Press, Delhi.

MEMOIRS OF THE REVOLUTION IN BENGAL
Author: John Campbell ,William Watts

MEMOIRS

OF THE

REVOLUTION

IN

BENGAL.

MEMOIRS

OF THE

REVOLUTION

IN

BENGAL,

ANNO. DOM. 1757.

By which MEER JAFFEIR was raised to the Government of that Province, together with those of *Babar* and *Orixa*.

INCLUDING

The Motives to this Enterprize; the Method in which it was accomplished; and the Benefits that have accrued from thence to that Country, our United Company trading to the *East Indies*, and to the *British* Nation.

LONDON:

PREFACE.

THE Succeſs that has every where attended the Efforts of the *Britiſh* Arms, during the Courſe of this juſt and neceſſary War, will render this Period of our Hiſtory reſplendent, even to lateſt Ages. It ſeems, therefore, requiſite to give the moſt accurate and diſtinct Accounts that can be obtained of theſe Succeſſes in the remoter Parts of the Globe, that the Nature and Conſequences of them may be the better under-

understood here. The People of *Britain* are as well entitled to know, and will with equal Pleasure read, what has been effected for their Service at *Bengal*, as at *Goree*; and accept as kindly the Laurels brought them from *Asia*, as those that come from *Afric* or *America*.

In this we follow only the Custom of other Nations. The *Portuguese* and the *Dutch* have not only general Histories of their Atchievements in the *Indies*, and separate Accounts of their respective Settlements, but numerous Memoirs of particular Expeditions, in which they have been exceeded by the *French*. We should therefore be wanting to ourselves, if, having performed as great Things as they, and having as authentic Vouchers, we should willfully suffer the

Memory

Memory of them to be loſt, and the Merits of our deſerving Countrymen ſwallowed up in Oblivion..

The following Pages will ſhew, how one of our fineſt Settlements in the *Eaſt Indies* was ſuddenly ſacked and ſubverted by the Impetuoſity of a young Man, intoxicated with Sovereign Power; in what Manner it was recovered and reſtored; the Peril to which it was again expoſed from the ſame Perſon; and the Means by which it was not only reſcued from a Second Deſtruction, but the Cauſes of theſe Calamities removed; the *Britiſh* Intereſt placed on a more ſold Baſis than ever; with additional Advantages that were never hoped; ſo that Stability may be truly ſaid to have been extracted from inteſtine Troubles, and Public Miſeries rendered

dered the Source of Public Safety and Public Benefits.

But as these Wonders could never have been performed but by the Assistance of his Majesty's Fleets and Forces, and as this was derived from the constant and laudable Concern of the Administration, for the Fate of *British* Subjects wherever disposed, it is but a just Tribute of Gratitude to shew how Measures so wisely taken, proved so successful in the Event, that Posterity may profit by the Example, and our Trade ever meet with the like Support, under Officers (if they are to be found) of equal Abilities.

Lastly, it will appear how far the Nation has reaped the Fruits of these signal Events. The Settlement at *Cal-*

Calcutta being not only effectually reftored, but, as far as the Nature of Things will admit, its future Safety as effectually fecured, the Honour of the *Britifh* Name repaired, and the Terror of her Arms diffufed throughout the *Eaft*. The Fortunes of *Britifh* Subjects, ruined in the firft Calamity, unprovided for in the firft Treaty, entirely recovered by the Second; many of which being now brought over, are actually vefted in the Funds or Lands of *Great-Britain*.

MEMOIRS

OF THE

REVOLUTION in *BENGAL*.

THE late Revolution in *Bengal* is ſo extraordinary in its Nature, of ſuch immediate Conſequence to the *Eaſt India* Company, and may poſſibly be of ſuch Importance to the Nation, that a ſhort and perſpicuous Relation of this memorable Tranſaction cannot but be acceptable to the Public. Such a Relation will give a diſtinct Idea of Things, as to which the World has hitherto had but confuſed Notions; diſpoſe all Events relating thereto in their proper Places, ſo that their Motives and Conſequences may be clearly underſtood; and ſupply thoſe Chaſms, that diſturb the Order and deſtroy the Connection between the Narratives which have been written occaſionally of particular Points of Fact. Beſides, it will explain the Conduct of thoſe who have been chiefly inſtrumental in bringing ſuch an hazardous, as well as arduous Attempt as this to a happy Concluſion; will ſhew why it was thought neceſſary, and on what Account it was originally undertaken; the many, and ſome of them formidable, Obſtacles that were in the Way; and how theſe were either gradually removed, or gloriouſly overcome. In a Word, when thoroughly and circumſtantially explained, it will open as ſingular and ſurprizing a Scene to the View of the inquiſitive and judicious Reader, as perhaps he will find in any Hiſtory reſpecting our own Times, which, let me have Leave to ſay, are thoſe that concern us moſt.

But previous to the Narrative, it will be expedient to give a conciſe Account of the Inhabitants, and the State of the Government in that Country, where this ſurprizing Political Cataſtrophe ſell out; and without being well acquainted with which, theſe ſuccinct Memoirs would not only be leſs intelligible, but, which is yet worſe, would become alſo very liable to be miſunderſtood. The Nature of Things depends on their Properties, alike difcernable by all who will examine them with equal Care, and with the fame Degree of Attention. But the Nature of Facts is determined by the Circumftances that attend them; and if thefe be not fairly and fully reprefented, they muft be falfely, or at leaft imperfectly apprehended. In Cafes relative to the Alteration of States, a bare Recital of Events eftablifhes only what Alteration they produced, and does not at all inform us to what the Change was owing; gives us no Grounds to conclude, as to the Advantages or Difadvantages flowing from fuch a Mutation, and does not furnifh us with the Means of framing any probable Conjecture as to the Stability or Inftability of the New Government.

The two great Nations, inhabiting this Part of the *Indies*, differ widely from each other in their Complexions, Language, Manners, Difpofition, and Religion. The *Moguls (Moghuls)* who are commonly called *Moors* or *Moormen*, are a robuft, ftately, and, in refpect to the original Natives, a fair People. They fpeak what the *Englifh* in *India* commonly call the *Moors* Tongue, which is in truth the *Perfian*, or at leaſt a Dialect of the *Perſian*. They are naturally vain, affect Shew and Pomp in every thing, are much addicted to Luxury, fierce, oppreſſive, and, for the moſt part, very rapacious. In reſpect to Religion, they are *Mohammedans*; the common Sort of the Sect of *Omar* (in which they agree with the *Turks*), but thoſe of Superior Rank are moſtly of the Sect of *Ali* (which is followed by the *Perſians*), and ſome affect to be very devout. Theſe have the Dominion, and are poſſeſſed of all the Offices of Truſt and Power, in virtue of their Deſcent from the *Moguls*, whoſe Empire was eſtabliſhed by *Timûr*, commonly called *Tamerlane* in this Country; but they are now a very mixed People, compoſed of *Tartars*, *Arabs*, and *Perſians*; more eſpecially of the laſt mentioned Nation; who for various Reaſons have quitted their own Country, but chiefly for the Sake of that Favour and Preferment, which for many Ages they have met with at the Court of *(Dehli) Delly*. The *Gentoows*, or Native *Indians*, are of a ſwarthy Aſpect, as their proper Appellation *Hindu* implies; leſs warlike but more active and induſtrious than the *Moors*. They are a mild, ſubtle, frugal Race of Men, exceedingly ſuper-

ſuperſtitious, ſubmiſſive in appearance, but naturally jealous, ſuſpicious, and perfidious; which is principally owing to that abject Slavery they are kept in by the *Moors*; and their Vices are ſuch as innate Cunning, of which they have a great deal, ſuggeſts to counteract thoſe of their Maſters. They are divided into ſeveral Caſts or Tribes, of which the moſt noble is that of the *Bramins*, and there are alſo ſeveral Caſts of theſe. Their Religion is *Paganiſm*, groſs and abſurd among the Vulgar, but not ſo amongſt the wiſer and better Sort. Theſe Characters are not drawn through any Spirit of Prejudice or Partiality, but from Experience and Obſervation; and the Faults of both do not ſo much ariſe from any Want of Parts, or Defect in their natural Talents, as from their reſpective Conditions, and the barbarous Severity and perpetual Inſtability of their Governments.

The *Mogul*, or, as we commonly call him, the *Great Mogul*, is, according to the Conſtitution of *Indoſtan*, if Deſpotiſm can with any Propriety be ſtiled a Conſtitution, as abſolute as a Monarch can be. He is the ſole Poſſeſſor of Property, the ſingle Fountain of

Honour, and the ſupreme Oracle of Juſtice. The whole Country belongs to him; all Honours are Perſonal, are beſtowed by his Bounty, and reſumed at his Pleaſure; his Subjects having no other Laws than the Dictates of his Will. The Omrahs, or Great Lords of his Court, who diſcharge the high Offices in his Houſhold, exerciſe the Functions of Miniſters of State, or hold ſuperior Commands in his Armies, are all Creatures of his own, and ſo are the Governors of Provinces, ſtiled in the Language of the Country *Nabobs*, who have again leſſer Governments, to which they appoint, called *Phouſdaries*. Thus things actually ſtood under the long Reign of *Aurengzebe*, and under the ſhort one of his Son; but ſince the Days of his unfortunate Grandſon, *Mohammed Shah*, who was dethroned, and reſtored by *Thamas Kouli Khan*, the *Moguls* are no more than Shadows of what they were; and their Prerogatives become rather Sounds than Subſtance. Thoſe Emirs or Nabobs, who govern great Provinces, are ſtiled Subahs, which imports the ſame as Lord-Lieutenants or Vice-Roys. Theſe Vice-Roys have ever held their Provinces of the Mogul, by rendering him a yearly

yearly Tribute, and furnishing their Contingent of Troops, when demanded for his Service; each of them exacting the like Services from their subordinate Governments; in both the Nabobs and Phousdars were supreme, and executed a kind of Sovereign Authority, subject only to those from whom it was delegated, and by whom it might be again taken away when they thought fit. But now they affect a kind of Independence, send their Tribute to Court when they esteem it convenient, and that is but seldom: and devolve their Employments on their Heirs, who having immediate Possession of the Means, find no great Difficulty in getting themselves confirmed, by making proper Presents at *Delly*. If the Mogul attempts to depose any of them, the Person to whom he gives the Commission must raise an Army, and force a Passage to the Government bestowed upon him with his Sword. The same thing happens with regard to the Phousdars, removed by the Suba's; and hence the Confusions that ensue, whenever the Pretenders to the same Post (who are also sometimes supported, as their Interest leads them, by the different trading Nations upon the Coast) to gratify their Ambition,

tion, create implacable, ruinous, and endless civil Wars.

As to the *Gentoows*, though Multitudes of them live in the Cities and Provinces governed by the Officers of the Mogul, yet in the mountainous Countries, and in some others, there are many who still maintain their Freedom, or rather are Slaves to Princes of their own, stiled Rajahs, amongst whom the Mahah Rajah, or King of the Marattes, is the most powerful. His Subjects inhabit the Mountains to the South-East of *Goa*, and he has sometimes brought Armies of one Hundred, and sometimes of two Hundred Thousand Men into the Field, composed mostly of Horse. These, as well as the Troops of the lesser Rajahs, of whom there are many, are employed chiefly in predatory Expeditions, and by making very rapid Incursions, and no less rapid Retreats, do a great deal of Mischief in a very little time. This has induced some of the wisest amongst the Mogul Governors to consent to the Payment of an annual Tribute, stiled the Chout, amounting to a fourth Part of the Revenue of the Province, to prevent these Inroads. The Nabobs like-

wise

wiſe frequently entertain the Troops of theſe Rajahs in Pay, in order to increaſe the Strength of their own Armies. From this conciſe Account of Things, it will ſufficiently appear, that the Power of the Mogul is rather nominal than real; that a kind of Anarchy reigns through the Country; and that where there is any Thing that reſembles ever ſo imperfectly a Form of Government, it has Force for its Baſis, is ſupported by Fraud, and that in Fact there is hardly any ſuch thing as legal Authority ſubſiſting in any Part of the Empire; ſo that to meaſure the Rectitude of Men's Actions in ſuch a Country as this, and in relation to ſuch Governors as theſe, by the ſame Rules that take Place under regular Eſtabliſhments, where Laws are ſettled and known, and where Juſtice is duly adminiſtred, is not at all founded either in Reaſon or Equity.

The Engliſh eſtabliſhed their Preſidency at *Calcutta*, towards the Cloſe of the laſt Century, in virtue of a Phirmaund (Firmân) from the famous *Aurengzebe*, who much extended the Bounds of the Empire on this Side. His Firmân was confirmed, and the Privileges

of

of the *East India* Company much augmented by his great Grandſon *Mohammed Furruksîr*. It is therefore indubitable, that having theſe Conceſſions made to them in the moſt ample and honourable Manner, and when the *Mogul* Empire was in its moſt flouriſhing Condition, the *Engliſh* Nation had as firm and ſolid a Right to their Poſſeſſions and Immunities as that Conſtitution could give. They were not therefore certainly to be diſturbed or controuled by the Governor of the Province, while they behaved themſelves peaceably and properly towards him.

The Company and the Servants of the Company had ſtrictly obſerved the Terms upon which they were beſtowed, and were ſo modeſt, or rather ſo cautious, as to keep much within the Bounds of thoſe Conceſſions, and choſe rather to wave ſome of their Rights than run the Hazard, under ſo unſettled a Government, of affording any Colour of Complaint. The ſame Spirit prevailed; the ſame Care was taken in all the Factories ſubordinate to this Preſidency. When Injuries were done them, they applied to the Suba's for Relief; when the Officers of thoſe Vice-Roys, either with or or without their Knowlege, ventured upon Exactions, they proceeded by Remonſtrance. If this had its Effect, they thought themſelves happy; if not, they bore it with Patience, of which many Inſtances might be given. They knew very well that Trade was their Buſineſs, and that Diſputes with the Country Government muſt be detrimental to their Intereſts; and therefore ſtudied to avoid them. That this was really the Caſe, that they had no ambitious Views, that they had not the ſmalleſt Intention to perplex or to interfere with the late Suba, appears to Demonſtration, from his not attempting to fix any ſuch thing upon them; and ſtill more ſo, from the Condition in which he found them.

The old Suba of the three Provinces of *Bengal*, *Bahar*, and *Orixa*, who had advanced himſelf, and ſeized that Dignity in the uſual Way, by a fortunate Audacity, ſticking at nothing to gratify his Thirſt for Power, *Aliverdy Cawn*, died much advanced in Years, *April* the 9th, 1756, and was ſucceeded by his adopted Son *Suraja Dowlat* (*Sur Rajah al Dowlat*) who began his Adminiſtration with Acts of Violence, and Breach of Faith to ſome

of

of his own Family; and by that time he had been a Month in Poſſeſſion of the high Office he aſſumed, manifeſted his Averſion to the *Engliſh*.

On what his Reſentment to the *Britiſh* Nation was founded, he was himſelf at a Loſs to ſay; and the trivial, inconſiſtent, and in various reſpects ill-grounded Pretences, he afterwards ſuggeſted, as the Motives to his Conduct, evidently ſhew they were contrived rather to hide, than to declare the Intentions from which he really acted. It has been aſſerted, and very probably not without ſufficient Foundation, that ſome who knew his violent and rapacious Diſpoſition, made their Court to him, by repreſenting, that the *Europeans* ſettled in the Provinces he poſſeſſed were immenſely rich; that he might well expect conſiderable Sums from them to merit his Favour and Protection upon his Acceſſion to the Government; that he had a Force much more than was adequate to the cruſhing them abſolutely, if he ſo pleaſed; that by compelling them, under Colour of their coming as Merchants only into *Indoſtan*, to deſiſt from raiſing any new Fortifications, he would have them

them always at his Mercy; and that in order to ſucceed effectually, and with little Trouble, he ſhould, to prevent their making it a common Cauſe, break only with one Nation at a time; and firſt with the *Britiſh*, who could pay him beſt, and whoſe Submiſſion would prove an effectual Precedent to the *French* and *Dutch*. It is not unlikely, that the Authors of this Advice might alſo undertake to negotiate a Compromiſe at a proper Juncture. This, however, is certain; that, before he proceeded to Hoſtilities, he had determined to reduce *Calcutta*, and had taken all his Meaſures for that Purpoſe, and diſpoſed his Inſtruments properly with that View.

Caſſimbuzar being ſituated, as it were, at his Door, was of courſe the firſt attacked. He cauſed the Place to be inveſted on the Twenty-ſecond of *May*, by a numerous Body of Troops, and then invited Mr. *Watts*, who was Chief of the Factory, to a Conference, upon a Safe-Conduct. As the Place (in the Opinion of the beſt Judges) was indefenſible, and if it had been defenſible, was without a Garriſon; as in point of Ceremony it was the uſual Cuſtom for the Chief of that Factory to

com-

compliment every new Suba on his assuming that Office, and Mr. *Watts* had all imaginable Reason to hope a good Reception, he accepted that Invitation, and went to the Suba's Camp, where, contrary to his Faith, and in Breach of those Engagements which are in that Country held sacred, he seized and detained him, till by pursuing the same Conduct, and intermixing Fraud and Force against those who had not the Means, and perhaps were doubtful whether they had any Authority to resist, he possessed himself of *Cassimbuzar*, on the fourth of *June*, and then made no farther Secret of his Design to deprive the *English* of all their Settlements, to which, according to the Constitution of the *Mogul* Empire, they had a much better Right than he had to his Dominions. Thus the Troubles of *Bengal* were begun by him in whose Ruin they ended.

This Step taken, his next Enterprize was directly against *Calcutta*; to reduce which, the Suba marched with an Army of Seventy thousand Men, and, when he became Master of it, acted with a Degree of insolent Cruelty, of which the World is too well apprized already, to need any Detail of it here. Let it suffice

ſuffice then to ſay, that the Suba wreaked his Malice, for Vengeance it could not be ſtiled, upon a Multitude of innocent People, who had never given him the ſmalleſt Offence. Having deſtroyed the Place, recalled, and then again diſperſed the Inhabitants, and with the ſame lawleſs Violence extorted large Sums from the *French* and *Dutch* Factories, that he might ſeem to manifeſt a general Diſtaſte to *Europeans*, he returned to *Muxadavad* in Triumph.

He had full five Months from this Period to recollect himſelf, and to conſider the Effects of theſe bold and arbitrary Proceedings, and in which he might have concerted either the Means of reſtoring the Peace of the Province, or of fortifying his own Strength in ſuch a manner as to be able to make Head againſt all his Enemies; for he began to find, that beſides thoſe this wanton Exerciſe of his Power had excited, he had ſeveral amongſt ſuch as had been ſubject to the Authority, and even ſincerely attached to the Perſon of his Predeceſſor. But his extreme Haughtineſs, and his perpetual Suſpicions, joined to the natural Mutability of his Temper, and Want of Experience,

perience, being a very young Man, rendered him equally incapable of correcting paſt Errors, or of digeſting any well-connected Plan, and ſupporting it with that Firmneſs, without which Succeſs is not to be expected. Sometimes obſtinate, moſtly irreſolute, he forfeited equally the Eſteem of Foreigners and Neighbours; and by an unaccountable Compound of Fickleneſs and Severity, loſt the Confidence of all, and excited the Secret Hatred of moſt of thoſe who were about him.

On the Fifth of *December* Admiral *Watſon* anchored with his Squadron in *Ballaſore* Road, to which Place Mr. *Watts* and Mr. *Becher*, both Gentlemen of the Council, were ſent to congratulate his Arrival, and to acquaint him with the Situation of their Affairs; Mr. *Watts* having been releaſed by the Nabob in *July*. Ten Days after the Squadron arrived at *Fulta*, where, without Loſs of Time, Meaſures were concerted for retrieving the Honour of the *Engliſh* Nation, and reſtoring the Affairs of the Company. The Force was not great, but it was directed by Men of determined Courage, and of diſtinguiſhed Capacities. Admiral *Watſon*, and the Commander in Chief of the

the Land Forces, Colonel *Clive*, who, after performing Wonders in other Parts of the *Indies*, came to perform ſtill greater Wonders here, and brought with him a Reputation that abundantly ſupplied the Want of Numbers. On the Twenty-eighth, the Fleet proceeded up the River. On the Twenty-ninth, Colonel *Clive* landed; and the very next Day, with the Aſſiſtance of the Squadron, made himſelf Maſter of the Fort of *Buſbudgia*; which, though a Place of great Strength, if it had been well defended, was taken with little Loſs, and proved the happy Omen of all the mighty Things which afterwards followed.

On New-Year's-Day, 1757, ſome of his Majeſty's Ships cannonaded the Batteries, which had been conſtructed by the Enemy for the Defence of *Calcutta*, where they had a conſiderable Force; and this with ſuch Succeſs, that when the Troops debarked, they were abandoned. On the Second, the *Engliſh* re-poſſeſſed themſelves of their demoliſhed Settlement; finding in the Fort, as they had done on the Batteries, a numerous Artillery left behind, by thoſe, who had not either Skill or Courage to uſe them. After this Succeſs, it was reſolved to proceed up the River to *Hughley*, a very populous Town, full of Warehouſes and Magazines; and in that, as well as other reſpects, a Place of Conſequence; and ſo much the ſafer from our Naval Force, as it could not be reached by large Ships. On the Fifth, Captain *Smith* in the *Bridgewater*, and the Sloop of War, anchored within Reach, and fired warmly upon the Town; and being ſeconded by all the armed Boats in the Fleet, it was very ſoon reduced. The better to diſtreſs the Enemy, the more to alarm the Province, and to work upon the Suba's governing Paſſion, Fear; Orders were given, though with much Reluctance, for burning the Houſes, and for deſtroying, particularly, all the Magazines on both Sides of the River; which Orders were very punctually executed, and thereby ſpeedily produced the deſired Effects.

Both Vice-Admiral *Watſon* and Colonel *Clive* had written, towards the Cloſe of the preceding Year, in as civil and polite Terms to the Suba, as the Circumſtances of Things would allow, with a View to bring about a Treaty. But that Prince, who had an Army about

about him, and whoſe Reſentments ran as high as ever, was either not inclined, or did not care to ſhew an Inclination, to come to any Terms. It was this, that made the Expedition to *Hughley* requiſite; and upon the Loſs of that, and the Supplies he had there, his Confidence immediately abated, and he condeſcended to anſwer the Letters, affirming that he had already written, but that he had Reaſon to believe, thoſe Letters had not been delivered. Yet even now, when he found it was neceſſary to offer a Negotiation, and to expreſs a Willingneſs to reinſtate the Company in their Factories, he added, as if requiſite to ſupport his Character, that if the *Engliſh* thought they could reap greater Benefits by purſuing the War, they might ſtill proceed in their military Operations; as if, by this Appearance of Indifference, he could conceal the Terror he was under, from what had already happened. To ſupport this Air of Intrepidity, he made, at the ſame Time, a Motion with his Army towards *Calcutta*.

Colonel *Clive* having communicated theſe Propoſals to the Select Committee, entruſted with the Management of the Affairs of the Factory, they ſent Meſſieurs *Walſh* and *Scrafton*, as Deputies, to the Camp of the Suba, who, either deceived by this into an Opinion that he was ſtill formidable to the *Engliſh*, or deſirous of impoſing upon the Deputies, behaved towards them with ſuch a Mixture of Haughtineſs and Contempt, as gave little Hopes of their making any great Progreſs in their Buſineſs; and therefore, after ſome Delay, the Vice-Admiral and the Colonel were obliged to reſume their former Meaſures, and to think of making a freſh Impreſſion on the Suba, that might convince him, he had as much to dread from the Land-Forces as the Fleet. In order to this, it was concerted, that a Detachment of Seamen, commanded by Captain *Warwick*, ſhould land and join the Army, and that Colonel *Clive* ſhould then force the Nabob's Camp. The Captain accordingly debarked, upon the Fifth of *February*, about One in the Morning: At Two they came up with the Forces, which were under Arms. By Three, every Thing was in Order, and they began to move towards the Enemy; the Sailors attending the Train, which conſiſted of Six Field Pieces, and one Haubitzer. About Five,

Five, the Action began, and the Artillery playing on the Right and Left, Colonel *Clive* marched his Troops directly through the Camp of the Suba; though he had between Forty and Fifty thousand Men, and obliged him, with great Loss, to dislodge, and even to abandon some of the Posts that he took after his Retreat; and this, with very little Detriment to his very small Army, not above Forty Men being killed, and not so many as Seventy wounded. This brisk Attack, seconded by a Letter from Vice-Admiral *Watson*, intimating, that this was a Specimen only of what the *British* Arms, when provoked, could perform, answered the Intention perfectly. The Suba immediately desired to renew the Negotiation, which went on with such Alacrity, that it was concluded and signed upon the Ninth, by which an end was put to a War, that had subsisted about Nine Months. This Treaty was conceived in the following Terms.

I. Whatever Rights and Privileges the King has granted the *English* Company, in their Phirmaund, and the Hushulhoorums sent from *Delly*, ſhall not be diſputed, or taken from them; and the Immunities therein mentioned, be acknowledged and ſtand good. Whatever Villages are given the Company by the Phirmaund, ſhall likewiſe be granted, notwithſtanding they have been denied by former Subahs. The Zemindars of thoſe Villages not to be hurt or diſplaced, without Cauſe.

Signed by the Nabob, in his own Hand.

I agree to the Terms of the Phirmaund.

II. All Goods paſſing and repaſſing through the Country, by Land or Water, with *Engliſh* Duſticks, ſhall be exempt from any Tax, Fee, or Impoſition whatever.

I agree to this.

III. All the Company's Factories, ſeized by the Nabob, ſhall be returned. All Monies, Goods, and Effects, belonging to the Company, their Servants and Tenants, and which have been ſeized and taken by the Nabob,

Nabob, ſhall be reſtored; what has been plundered and pillaged by his People, made good by the Payment of ſuch a Sum of Money, as his Juſtice ſhall think reaſonable.

I agree to reſtore whatever has been ſeized and taken by my Orders, and accounted for in my Sincary.

IV. That we have Permiſſion to fortify *Calcutta*, in ſuch Manner as we may think proper, without Interruption.

I conſent to this.

V. That we ſhall have Liberty to coin Siccas, both of Gold and Silver, of equal Weight and Fineneſs with thoſe of *Muxadavad*, which ſhall paſs in the Provinces.

I conſent to the Engliſh *Company's coining their own Imports of Bullion and Gold into Siccas.*

VI. That a Treaty ſhall be ratified, by Signing and Sealing, and ſwearing to abide by the Articles therein contained; not only by the Nabob, but his principal Officers and Miniſters.

I have ſealed and ſigned the Articles, before the Preſence of God.

VII. That Admiral *Watſon* and Colonel *Clive*, on the Part and Behalf of the *Engliſh* Nation, and of the Company, do agree to live in a good Underſtanding with the Nabob, to put an End to theſe Troubles, and to be in Friendſhip with him, while theſe Articles are performed and obſerved by the Nabob.

I have ſealed and ſigned the foregoing Articles, upon theſe Terms, that if the Governor and Council will ſign and ſeal them, with the Company's Seal, and will ſwear to the Performance on their Part, I then conſent and agree to them.

In this Treaty, the intelligent Reader will ſee, there were Three great Points ſufficiently explained, to ſhew the Injuſtice and Oppreſſion of the Suba, in his Attack upon the *Engliſh* Settlements, even upon Reflection in his own Opinion, tho' far from being as con-
clusive

clusive in respect to the Remedies and Indemnifications, that, in consequence of so full a Declaration, were to be procured. The First regarded the Possessions, Immunities, and Privileges, conceded to the *East India* Company, by the Royal Phirmaund, which *Suraja Dowlat* acknowleged to have violated, promised Restitution, and undertook, in the most solemn Manner, not to invade them again. But as this was conceived only in general Terms, these Rights, and the Limits of their respective Possessions, required a thorough Discussion. The next was, as to the Fortifications of *Calcutta*; the Legality and Expediency of which he now admitted in their utmost Extent, as being plainly necessary to the Security of the Place, the *British* Inhabitants, and even of the *Mogul*'s Subjects, living under its Protection; and to this was added, the Coinage of their own Imports, in Gold and Silver, to which they had always a Right, though it had not been exercised. The last was, the full and immediate Compensation, which he stipulated, for all the Damages the Company, and those dependent upon it, had sustained; but which he contracted only to make, so far as the Produce

Produce of the Plunder ſhould appear to have come into his Hands. It was evident, therefore, that, though in Words and in Appearance much had been obtained by the Peace, this ſtill depended, in a great Meaſure, as to the moſt material Part, the Performance, on the proper Settling of theſe Articles, and the Liquidation of the Damages, in reference to which, the Sincerity of the Suba's Intention, and his Readineſs to execute what he had undertaken, was almoſt the ſole Security. In order to adjuſt theſe Points, without which the Treaty was of very little Conſequence to thoſe ruined and undone by the War, the Select Committee very properly made choice of Mr. *William Watts*, who had been their Chief at *Caſſimbuzar*, who was one of the Members of that Committee, a Perſon well known to the Nabob, and who had been, as the Suba himſelf owned, the firſt innocent and cauſeleſs Victim to his Reſentment, or rather Caprice. His Acceptance of this Commiſſion, by which he was again to put himſelf into the Power of this unſteady Prince, in ſo critical a Conjuncture, and charged with ſo troubleſome and intricate a Negotiation, was a very full Proof of his Fide-

Fidelity to, and Zeal for, the Intereſts of the Company; as it likewiſe was an evident Teſtimony of the good Opinion of his Aſſociates; who, upon mature Deliberation, inveſted him ſolely with ſo great a Truſt.

He was, indeed, in every reſpect, fitteſt for this Employment (had there been any Competitor); an Employment, by far the weightieſt, and of the moſt Conſequence, of any in *Bengal*. He had been many Years in the Country; was well acquainted with the Language, as well as accuſtomed to the Manners and Diſpoſition of the Inhabitants; was much eſteemed, and had many Connections with them. He underſtood their Politics alſo, at leaſt as much as ſuch fluctuating Politics as theirs could be underſtood; the true Intereſt of the Province, and the Conſtitution of *Indoſtan* in general, and the State of the neighbouring Governments in particular. Beſides, he was perſonally known to all the Miniſters, and had received very ſingular Marks of Eſteem from the Suba himſelf. Add to all this, that the Company, in caſe of the Death or Reſignation of Mr. *Drake*, had appointed this Gentleman to the Government of *Calcutta*, which, taken together, proves, that this Choice was not the Work of Chance or Favour, but proceeded from mature Deliberation, and a juſt Regard to the Conſequence of that Negotiation, in which he was to be employed.

The Perplexities ſpringing from ſuch a Variety and Complication of Matters that were to be adjuſted, the Mutability of the Suba's Nature, and his Want of Judgment and Experience, and the Difficulties naturally ariſing in ſettling the Conceſſions, which had been juſt extorted from him by Treaty, were not the only Circumſtances that embarraſſed this Negotiation. The *French*, perfectly well informed of every Step taken or intended, and no leſs ſkilled in the Art of Intrigue, had moſt effectually retained ſeveral of thoſe whom the Suba frequently conſulted, or chiefly truſted, in their Intereſt by gratifying them with Preſents. They had ſtill a more powerful Tie on them than this, being in Debt Thirteen Lack of Rupees, or upwards of One hundred and Sixty thouſand Pounds Sterling, to *Juggut Seat*, the greateſt Banker in the Empire of *Indoſtan*, and the Second in Power

in

in *Bengal*; to whoſe Advice for many Years paſt the Subas paid the greateſt Attention. They very well knew, that Men might be falſe to their Benefactors; but they rightly judged, that even the worſt of Men, more eſpecially when avaricious, would be true, where they could not poſſibly be falſe, without betraying their own Intereſt. Under Circumſtances like theſe, there was no Probability, indeed there was no Poſſibility, of ſo much as attempting any Thing, but in the Mode of the Court; that is, by oppoſing Corruption to Corruption, making Friends of the Mammon of Unrighteouſneſs, and getting upon even Ground with thoſe, with whom they were obliged to contend.

But in order to underſtand the whole of this Matter thoroughly, we muſt conſider the State that Affairs were then in, with reſpect to the two contending Nations. Advice of the breaking out of the War, between *Great Britain* and *France*, arrived in *India*, the very Day after the Treaty was concluded with the Suba; and of courſe opened a new Scene. From being commercial and political Rivals, we were now become open Enemies; a Circumſtance

cumſtance which we were very ſure the *French* would improve, and which therefore it was our Duty not to neglect. We had at preſent a Fleet and an Army; for however ſmall they might be, as Matters ſtood, they both deſerved thoſe Titles, and this gave us great Advantages. On the other Hand, the former was ſoon to quit the Coaſt, and perhaps Part of the latter, which was a great Diſadvantage. The capital Point, therefore, was to avail ourſelves of them, while they remained, ſo as to ſettle Things upon a ſtable Foundation, with regard to the *French*, as well as to the Nabob, before the Seaſon came in which the Fleet was to return. In reſpect to the former, the Admiral and Colonel *Clive*, with the Aſſiſtance of the Select Committee, were to take the beſt Meaſures they could; and Mr. *Watts* was to regulate the latter; and his Succeſs, or Want of Succeſs, muſt have apparently had ſuch an Influence upon the whole, that the Reader moſt certainly needs not be informed, how much depended upon his Courage, Conduct, and Capacity.

The Intereſt the *French* had in the Court

of the Suba, and their Method of acquiring it, have been already ſtated. This they would have underſtood to be barely for their own Support and Security; but however, there were ſome Surmiſes, that it was alſo, and had ever been, not a little to our Prejudice. It was whiſpered, that the Favour ſhewn them, in Compariſon of the *Dutch*, after the Deſtruction of our Settlements, when he affected to fine both Nations for augmenting the Works about their reſpective Factories, was, in Conſideration of their having ſecretly furniſhed Artillery, when he marched againſt *Calcutta*. This was a Suſpicion in the *Indies*, and as ſuch only is mentioned; but it is very certain, that the Letters wrote Home to *Europe* were entirely in *Suraja Dowlat*'s Favour, containing a very unfair, and, which was much worſe, a very plauſible, but utterly falſe Repreſentation of the Grounds of the Quarrel, which was publiſhed to our Prejudice in all the foreign Gazettes.

When Mr. *Watts* ſet out for the Suba's Reſidence, he was accompanied by *Omichund*, an eminent Merchant of *Calcutta*, who was well

well known to the Suba, and his Ministers. This Merchant, Mr. *Watts* sent to *Hughley*, to discover, as far as he could, what were the real Intentions of the *Moors*, in case we attacked *Chandenagore*. He returned the next Day, *February* the Eighteenth, with a very distinct Account. He had been informed by *Nuncomar*, the Phousdar, or Governor of *Hughley*, that the very Day before, Two Persons, *Seen Bawboo* and *Montra Mull*, arrived from the Nabob, with a Lack of Rupees, as a Present to the *French* Factory; and also with Orders to the Phousdar, to assist the *French*, if attacked; or if they were the Aggressors, to assist the *English*. Mr. *Watts* was too well acquainted with the Genius of the *Moors*, and the Temper of the Suba, to be deceived by this Shew of Impartiality. He considered the Present as a Declaration in Favour of the *French*; and the Stile of his Orders as calculated to amuse the *English*. *Omichund* was entirely of the same Opinion. Mr. *Watts*, therefore, advised the Select Committee to attack *Chandenagore* without Delay, assuring them, that they had nothing to apprehend from the Resentment of the Suba; that if once the two Nations were engaged

in

in Hoſtilities, the *Moors* would not come to the Succour of either; and that after all, there were but Three hundred Matchlock Men in *Hughley*. He ſaw from the Beginning the Michief that was to be feared; and the only Remedy that could be applied. He therefore very freely pointed out the one, and very warmly recommended the other. It had been a very happy Event, if his Counſel had been then taken.

On the Twenty-firſt of *February*, in the Evening, Mr. *Watts* arrived in the Camp, and had his Audience of the Suba, who embraced him, gave him the ſtrongeſt Aſſurances that every thing ſhould be adjuſted ſpeedily, and to his Satisfaction; adding a Promiſe of the Surpau, (Sirrapah) or Veſt of Honour, which, however, Mr. *Watts* declined receiving, till they came to *Muxadavad*. He was very ſoon ſenſible of the Difficulty of his Taſk, the Pains he muſt be at in tracing the Goods taken from their ſeveral Factories, the procuring actual Reſtitution in ſome Caſes, an equitable Equivalent in others; the reſtoring a free Commerce, which had been ſtopped, by expreſs Orders, from the very Beginning of the

Troubles; and in doing all this, of the almoſt inſurmountable Obſtacles that the Mutability of the Suba's Inclinations, the Intrigues of the *French*, the Inſinuations of Miniſters, ſwayed ſolely by their own Intereſts, would throw in his Way. But he ſaw, that the true Source of all theſe Embarraſſinents was the Suba's Inſincerity, and the Scheme he had formed of reſuming his Deſpotiſm, in regard to the *Europeans*, by borrowing their own Aſſiſtance, and playing one Nation againſt another, till, by the weakening of their Forces in ſuch Diſputes, he became too ſtrong for both. His Project was too great for his Capacity; he did what he could to execute it, but it was beyond his Force, and his very manner of managing it defeated his Deſign.

The public Declarations of this irreſolute Prince, were diametrically oppoſite to the whole Tenor of his Conduct. He had no ſooner concluded the Treaty with Us, than he wrote to Admiral *Watſon* in the warmeſt Terms of Friendſhip, and in a very remarkable Letter to Colonel *Clive* aſſures him, that our Enemies ſhould be his, as he expected that we ſhould look upon his Enemies as ours:

ours; and that he depended upon the Aſſiſtance of the *Engliſh* for maintaining the future Tranquility of his Dominions. But when Mr. *Watts* communicated to him at large the Reaſons that might induce us to reduce the *French* Settlement at *Chandenagore*, he made no Scruple of altering his Language. He then ſaid, he would not ſuffer the Peace of his Territories to be violated by either Nation; that he would protect both, while they remained quiet; that he would aſſiſt the *French* with all his Forces, if we, after this, ever attacked them; and that he would join us in like Manner, if we were attacked by the *French*. All this, however, was far from impoſing on thoſe who were at the Head of our Affairs. Mr. *Watts* framed his Precautions ſo well, that he knew exactly the Meaſures which the Suba took, or was inclined to take, and gave the moſt early Intelligence of them to the Select Committee, who, from thence, were well enabled to take their own; by which his Schemes were diſappointed without Noiſe, and without ſo much as ſuſpecting their having any ſuch Informations; though theſe came chiefly from his own Head-Spy, who, by an Application these Sort of People rarely can resist, Mr. *Watts* had brought over entirely to the Company's Interests.

By comparing his private Intrigues with some of his more public Transactions, there could not be a Shadow of Doubt left as to his real Intentions, though he always dissembled, and often disavowed them. Immediately after his Treaty with Us, and consequently after he knew that they were our Enemies, he bestowed upon them very conspicuous Marks of Kindness, and such as could not fail of affording Umbrage to the *English*. He made them, as has been before-mentioned, a Present of a Lack of Rupees in ready Money; he cancelled an Obligation they had given him for twice that Sum; he promised them the Privileges of a Mint; he proposed granting them a very considerable Augmentation of Territory; and even went so far, as to offer them the Possession of the City of *Hughley*. These were Circumstances that indicated their standing much in his good Graces, or that he expected from them Services equivalent to these substantial and extraordinary Benefits. The Truth, as far as it could

could ever be discovered, was this. They, and his Ministers in their Interest, made him believe their Strength in his Dominions to be very far beyond what it really was. Besides this, they magnified their Successes in other Parts, and took a great deal of Pains to persuade him, that Mr. *Bussy*, with a very numerous Army, was within a little Distance of his Territories, and might either fall upon, or come to his Support against, any Enemy, according as he should behave towards them. These Representations, the Nature of the Suba considered, may in some measure, and only in some measure, account for the Part that he acted.

As Mr. *Watts* was upon the Spot, watched every Motion of the Suba, knew exactly the Character of his Courtiers and principal Ministers, and had the most certain Intelligence of every thing that passed, he continued to represent the Necessity of attacking *Chandenagore*. He saw that, as far as his Timidity would suffer him to go, the Suba was already united to the *French*. He was satisfied that he dealt deceitfully with the *English*; more especially after Mr. *Watts* prevailed on Colonel *Clive* to write to the Suba, in the ſtrongeſt Terms, that he might confide in him on every Occaſion; and that on any Emergency he would march at his Requeſt to his Aſſiſtance, againſt all his Enemies. After this, the Suba never mentioned any Deſire or Thoughts of demanding Aid from the *Britiſh* Nation. Mr. *Watts* was therefore convinced that we could never gain him; and that, though now he temporized, he waited only a fit Seaſon to act againſt us, in Conjunction with the *French*, upon whom he was daily heaping Favours, while it was with much Difficulty, and in conſequence of repeated Sollicitations, he was ever brought to do common Juſtice to us. In this Situation Mr. *Watts* exhorted the Admiral, the Colonel, and the Select Committee, not to let ſlip this ſavourable Opportunity, and to apprehend nothing from the Suba's Reſentment, who would never venture to give them any Succours, or take an open Part in their Favour, or to our Prejudice. But if the Fleet was once gone, and a fair Occaſion offered, he would as certainly embrace it, and begin a new War, with as little Scruple as he had done the laſt, with more Advan-

tage

tage on his Side, and leſs on ours: Arguments, which, though ſtrong and ſelf-evident, did not meet with general Acceptance.

The Select Committee, though they paid great Deference to the Advice, and had a very juſt Senſe of the Zeal, of Mr. *Watts*, for the Nation and the Company's Service; yet they were very unwilling to venture again upon Hoſtilities, from a ſtrong Suſpicion that the Suba, whether he actually joined the Enemy or not, would ſuſpend the Execucution of the Treaty, renew the Interruption of their Trade, and by that Means hinder their Inveſtments for another Year. They knew ſo well, and dreaded ſo much, the Conſequences that would have inevitably attended ſuch an Event, that, in ſpite of all Mr. *Watts* could allege, they inclined to a Neutrality. This was an Expedient the Suba had propoſed, and was another viſible Indication of what were his ſecret and ſettled Intentions. The Sentiments, or rather the Sollicitations of the Select Committee, prevailed upon the Admiral and the Colonel to acquieſce in this Plan; inſomuch that the latter wrote in very ſtrong and pathetic Terms to the Suba, informing him, that whatever Repreſentations of a contrary Nature he might have received, yet himſelf was very confident, that his Forces were able to reduce *Chandenagore* in Two days; nevertheleſs, in conſideration of the great Repugnancy he ſhewed to the diſturbing the Tranquility of the Province, he would, out of pure Regard to the Suba's Friendſhip, conſent to ſuch a Neutrality as he propoſed, provided it was guarantied by him, and he ſolemnly undertook to act with all his Forces againſt that Nation by which it was firſt infringed.

When Mr. *Watts* ſaw, that after all he had offered againſt it, this Point was driven thus far, and that in all Probability it would be ſpeedily concluded, he turned his Thoughts to the giving it ſtill greater Security, and with that View adviſed, that *Juggut Seat* ſhould undertake for the due Performance of whatever ſhould be agreed upon by the *French*; which, conſidering the Influence that his Debt gave him over them, and the high Credit in which he ſtood with the Suba and his Miniſters, appeared to be the only Method of giving to this Meaſure the utmoſt Conſiſt-

ency

ency of which it was capable. This ſhews how perfectly well-diſpoſed Mr. *Watts* was to facilitate any Step taken for the Company's Service, though ever ſo contrary to his own Opinion; and at the ſame Time affords a Proof of his thorough Knowlege of Men and Things in that Country, by which he was enabled to deviſe the Means of rendering this Convention more ſafe and more effectual, than any that had been propoſed by ſuch as had originally planned, and now preſſed its Execution. But though he diſcovered ſo much Integrity, and ſo much Abilities in ſuggeſting this additional Strength to a Neutrality, he ſtill looked upon it as diametrically oppoſite to the Company's true Intereſt, and as the ſingle Step that could ever put it in the Power of the Suba and the *French*, to bring their deep and dangerous Deſigns to bear.

But when all ſeemed to be abſolutely ſettled, and nothing wanting to this Neutrality but the concluding and ſigning it in Form, the *French* themſelves overturned it, by avowing that they had no ſufficient Authority to ſupport an Act of that Nature, which might be declared invalid by their Superiors. Mr. *Watts* im-

immediately laid hold on and improved this very unexpected Incident, by reprefenting, in the ftrongeft Light, to the Suba, the Condefcenfion fhewn him by the *Britifh* by accepting, and the Indignity offered to him by the *French* in rejecting, his Expedient. This had fo great an Effect, that in the firft Tranfport of his Refentment he directed a Letter to be written to Vice-Admiral *Watfon*, in which he tacitly permitted the Attack of the *French* Factory, by recommending Mercy to the Enemy when it fhould be reduced; and defiring the military Operations of the *Englifh* might be conducted with as little Prejudice to his Country, or Difturbance to his People, as it was poffible. Mr. *Watts*, who had fecured the Suba's Secretary to our Intereft, engaged him to pen this important Epiftle in a proper Stile, fo as to permit the Attack immediately, and to difpatch it without Delay: Precautions, which were of the utmoft Confequence, and which, in the Event, gave us all thofe Advantages we afterwards reaped, and which, through the Bleffing of Divine Providence, we ftill poffefs in *Bengal*.

As there was great Addrefs ufed in obtaining

taining this Letter, ſo it arrived in the moſt critical Conjuncture. For, notwithſtanding the *French* had avowed their Want of Power to conclude an effectual Neutrality, yet ſo much were ſome afraid of recurring again to Arms, that they were ſtill for accepting of this Expedient, however precarious. Upon this, Admiral *Watſon* held a Council of War, to conſider what was moſt proper to be done; and it was while this Council was actually ſitting, wherein thoſe who argued yet for a Neutrality inſiſted chiefly upon the Suba's Repugnancy to ſee the Flame of War, ſo lately extinguiſhed, again rekindled in his Dominions, that this Letter was brought, which cut the Gordian Knot, and put an End to the Debate. How the *French* came to act in this Manner, and by ſo frank a Declaration defeat the Scheme of the Suba, and run themſelves upon Deſtruction, is not eaſy to conceive. In all Probability, they did not imagine, that even, after this, we would venture to fall upon them, and they were willing to preſerve to themſelves, againſt a proper Seaſon, the Liberty of attacking us; or, which is yet more probable, depended on the Suba's exerting his whole Force, in Caſe of

our

our besieging them, in their Defence; which would have rendered the Expedition much more difficult. Be this as it will, the Letter defeated all their Schemes; and the Sequel of the Transaction shewed how much better Mr. *Watts* was acquainted with the Disposition of the *Moors*, and more thoroughly Master of the Suba's Temper, and Manner of acting, notwithstanding the Intrigues they had been so long carrying on in his Court, and their having such Connections with his Favourites and Ministers.——But let us now return from Reflections to Facts, and having clearly stated this very remarkable Stroke of Policy, resume the Thread of our Narrative.

Vice-Admiral *Watson*, Colonel *Clive*, and the Select Committee, came to this final Resolution, in the Beginning of the Month of *March*, and entered with all the Diligence and Dispatch possible on the necessary Preparations for this important Expedition, well knowing that the *French* were not ignorant of their own Danger, or at all remiss or careless in providing against it. *Chandenagore*, the chief of their Settlements in *Bengal*, was a Place very well situated on the Side of the River

River, Twenty-ſeven Miles above *Calcutta*, which is a Branch of the *Ganges*, at a ſmall diſtance below *Hughley*. The Director at this Settlement has under him the *French* Company's Factories of *Caſſimbuzar*, *Dacca*, *Patna*, *Jeuda*, and *Ballaſore*. They prudently contrived, at the Beginning of the Troubles, to ſtrengthen it with various Outworks and Batteries, had in it a Garriſon of Five hundred *Europeans* and Seven hundred *Blacks*, with ſome Mortars, and near Two hundred Pieces of Cannon mounted. They took the Precaution alſo to ſend away ſome of their Merchandize, and the beſt Part of their Effects, under Colour of providing the better for their Defence; raiſed conſiderable Magazines, which were well provided; and made ſuch Diſpoſitions, and kept ſo good a Countenance, as impoſed upon moſt of the *Moors*, and perhaps upon ſome of themſelves. As they chiefly feared the Squadron, they ſunk Two Ships, a Ketch, a Hulk, a Snow, and a Veſſel without Maſts, directly in the Channel, within Gunſhot of the Fort, and laid Two Booms, moored with Chains, acroſs the River. Beſides theſe, they ſunk and ran on Shore Five large Veſſels, above the Fort, that they might throw

throw every Impediment possible in the Way of our Squadron. In consequence of these military Operations, which were very judiciously planned, and the best their Circumstances would admit, they resolved to stand the Attack; but whether they had any Hopes given them by the Suba of his Assistance, or whether they relied at all on his Insinuations of Aid, in case they were given, could not be learned; though he actually advanced a Corps of Troops, as we shall see hereafter, which might render such a Conjecture not at all improbable.

A Reinforcement of Three hundred Men from *Bombay* arriving at *Calcutta*, Colonel *Clive* advanced by the River Side, with Seven hundred Whites, and Sixteen hundred Seapoys, towards the *French* Settlement; and with very little Loss took Possession of most of the Out-Posts on the Fourteenth of *March*. On the Fifteenth, the Enemy abandoned all their Batteries, notwithstanding these were very well disposed, and in exceeding good Order. He was now possessed of every Post they had, but the Fort, and a Redoubt seated between the River Side and the Fort Walls, where-

wherein were mounted Eight Pieces of Cannon, Twenty-four Pounders, Four of which pointed down the River. The ſame Day Admiral *Watſon* ſailed with the *Kent* of Sixty-four, the *Tyger* and *Saliſbury*, each of Fifty Guns, having previouſly ſent a Twenty-Gun Ship, and a Sloop, to cover the Boats attending the Camp. On the Eighteenth, he anchored about Two Miles below *Chandenagore*, and the Troops on Shore being employed in raiſing a Battery againſt the Fort, the Weather becoming extremely foggy, and the Impediments before-mentioned being of Neceſſity to be removed, occaſioned ſome Delay. The Firſt Thing to be done was clearing the River; and the Booms being cut, and running adrift, a proper Paſſage was ſoon diſcovered, by ſounding, and without loſing Time in weighing the *French* Veſſels. While this was about, the brave Admiral *Pocock*, who was juſt arrived at *Culpee* in the *Cumberland*, reſolving to have a Share in the Action, came in his Long-Boat, and going on board his Majeſty's Ship the *Tyger*, hoiſted his Flag there. On the Twenty-third, at Six in the Morning, the *Tyger*, *Kent*, and *Saliſbury*, weighed.

weighed. About Ten Minutes after the Enemy began to fire from the Redoubt, but their Artillery was ſoon ſilenced by the *Tyger*. Before Seven the Ships were properly ſtationed, and the Signal being given, the Engagement began; the Firing continuing very briſk on both Sides, till a Quarter after Nine, when the Beſieged hung out a Flag of Truce, and the Articles of Capitulation were very quickly ſettled and ſigned. In conſequence of this, Captain *Latham*, of the *Tyger*, was diſpatched by Vice-Admiral *Watſon* to receive the Keys of the Fort, into which Colonel *Clive* marched with the Troops about Five in the Afternoon. Thus *Chandenagore*, according to the Scheme originally propoſed, conſtantly inſiſted upon, and at laſt rendered practicable by Mr. *Watts*, with all the *French* ſubordinate Settlements in the Province of *Bengal*, were reduced; and thereby moſt of the Schemes laid for the future Deſtruction of *Calcutta*, and the other *Engliſh* Factories, rendered abortive. An Expedition, in the firſt Inſtance, glorious to the *Britiſh* Arms, and in its Conſequences, as from the Sequel of this Relation will appear, of the higheſt Importance.

This

This ſignal Advantage was not obtained without ſome Loſs. Admiral *Pocock* was wounded, but not dangerouſly. The gallant Captain *Henry Speke*, equally diſtinguiſhed by the Clearneſs of his Head and the Warmth of his Heart, who commanded the *Kent*, on board which Vice-Admiral *Watſon* wore his Flag, received a Wound from a Cannon Shot, which unhappily carried away the Leg of his Son, who deceaſed ſoon after, a Youth of the moſt amiable Character, extraordinary Learning, and admirable Abilities. The firſt Lieutenant, Mr. *Samuel Perreau*, and the Maſter of the *Tyger*, were both killed; the Third and Fourth Lieutenants were alſo wounded; and the former died. Of the private Men there were Thirty-two killed, and One hundred wounded. The Enemy had Forty killed and Seventy wounded in the Fort. They muſt be allowed to have defended themſelves with great Spirit and Reſolution, and probably would not have ſubmitted ſo ſoon, if they had not ſuffered ſeverely from Colonel *Clive*'s Batteries, and been ſtill more galled by the Fire of his Men, from the flat Roofs of the Houſes, which in Truth made it almoſt impoſſible for them to ſtand to their

Guns. A Part of the *French* Troops made their Eſcape, and marched Northwards, after whom Colonel *Clive* ſent a Detachment of Six hundred Seapoys, and Vice Admiral *Watſon* ordered ſeveral Boats up the River of *Hughley*, to ſeize upon whatever was *French* Property; notwithſtanding which, a great deal of the Company's Effects and Merchandize were concealed and carried away. This Blow was very deciſive in reference to the *French*, whoſe Meaſures it entirely broke, by rendering the Schemes they had formed, with reſpect to the Suba, utterly impracticable. On the other hand, it releaſed the *Engliſh* from the Apprehenſions they were under of being again attacked in *Calcutta*, in caſe the Squadron had left them without reducing this Place. Theſe were ſo far from being Suſpicions lightly founded, that their Danger was ſo great and ſo apparent, conſidering the Circumſtances they were then in, and the Suba's delaying to reſtore their Artillery, that, if not encouraged by this Event, they would have been very ſlow in re-ſettling *Calcutta*. Happy as thoſe immediate Effects were! they were hardly ſo much as remembred, after the greater Advantages that followed; which de-

mon-

monſtrated how juſtly this Reſolution was taken, and in what a critical Conjuncture it was executed.

We have before hinted, that, notwithſtanding the Suba had tranſmitted a Letter of Permiſſion to Vice-Admiral *Watſon* to act as he thought proper againſt the *French*, without which Letter the Admiral and the Colonel would not have proceeded, nay went farther, and recommended them to his Mercy, yet he preſently changed his Mind. He deſired Mr. *Watts* to write to the Colonel, that he would not have War made in his Country, by which the People under his Government muſt ſuffer, the King's Revenues be leſſened, and the Tranquility of his Dominions diſturbed. The *French*, who had miſled him from the Beginning, deceived him to the very laſt. They aſſured him, that, in the firſt Attack, the *Engliſh* had been repulſed with Loſs, and gave him to underſtand, that they did not doubt obliging them to retire. The Suba was ſo much embarraſſed by the contradictory Reports he heard, and looked upon this Tranſaction to concern him ſo nearly, that he wrote Letter after Letter to Colonel

Clive, who is ſaid to have received no leſs than Ten of them in one Day, and theſe in very oppoſite Stiles; which the Colonel anſwered punctually, with all the Calmneſs and Complaiſance imaginable, expreſſing great Concern at the Impreſſion which the Calumnies of his Enemies had made on that Prince's Mind, and aſſuring him of his ſincere Attachment, as long as he adhered to the Treaty. At length the Suba grew ſo very uneaſy, that he ſent *Mutrumul*, in whom he ſaid he placed great Confidence, to the Colonel, with Orders to act, if there was any room for it, as a Mediator. But the Situation of Things at his Arrival made ſuch a Commiſſion viſibly impracticable; which *Mutrumul* perceiving, extolled the *Engliſh* highly, and threw all the Blame upon the *French*. To give Weight, however, to this intended Mediation, *Roydoolub* advanced, by his Maſter's Command, at the Head of Six thouſand Men, within a ſmall Diſtance of *Hughley*. But to prevent this from giving any Umbrage, *Mutrumul*, when the Attack was made, aſſured the Colonel, that *Roydoolub* had the Suba's Inſtructions to obey his Orders, which the Colonel took in exceeding good Part, and returned that Prince Thanks

Thanks for this gracious Offer of his Aſſiſtance. The Moment the Place ſurrendered, he gave Notice of it to the Suba, and aſcribed his Succeſs to the Favour of Heaven and his Excellency's Auſpice, under which his Arms had been ſo fortunate. A Compliment, which the Suba knew not how to receive with even a tolerable Grace, or to reject without giving Offence. In reality, he had brought his Affairs by this time into a very perplexed Condition, of which he was ſenſible, now it was too late; though very probably he might not have Sagacity enough to diſcern, that the Whole of theſe Misfortunes had no other Source than the Unſteadineſs of his Councils, and the Duplicity of his Conduct. What we have already ſaid will afford Proofs more than ſufficient to eſtabliſh this; but as the ſetting it in a clear Light will be the beſt means of explaining the Motives to the Tranſactions that enſued, we hope the ſubſequent Remarks will not appear tedious to the Reader.

The Suba, wanting alike in Parts and in Experience, unable to reject bad Counſels, and prone to purſue his own Notions, as far as they could be carried by his Power, ſhewed plainly from the very Beginning, that he had no formed Syſtem; and if he could be ſtiled ſo at all, was certainly a bad Politician. His ſetting out was by breaking at once with all the *European* Nations; which, if their reciprocal Jealouſies of each other, and ſome other Circumſtances, had not hindered, muſt have united them all againſt him, and that Union would have rendered his Scheme abortive. As this did not happen, it encouraged him to take another wrong Step, by attacking and deſtroying the *Engliſh*, without having ſo much as a plauſible Pretence. This Act of arbitrary Violence viſibly ſubverted the Foundation of his own Scheme, if it ever had any, by proving, in the ſtrongeſt Manner, that no *European* Nation could ſubſiſt as Merchants in his Dominions, without having Places ſo well fortified, as not to lie at his Mercy. When, therefore, he was reduced to the Neceſſity of concluding a Treaty, the very Baſis of that Treaty was his confeſſing this laſt Poſition to be well founded, and admitting by his own Conſent, as the only practicable Grounds of Peace, what he had before laid down as the Reaſon of his taking up Arms.

Arms. But when he had done this, and might have been quiet, by adhering conſtantly to that Treaty, he again miſtook his Point. Uniformity of Conduct was ſo little in his Conſtitution, that he immediately loſt all the Advantages he ſeemed to have ſought by that Meaſure, and which indeed were clearly aſſerted to have been the Objects he had in View, in his Letters to Admiral *Watſon* and Colonel *Clive*, by ſhewing a viſible Repugnance to the Execution of it in every Step, and doing that ſlowly and ungracefully, which, if he had done chearfully and at once, might have procured him the Confidence of the *Engliſh*, and have thoroughly extricated him from thoſe Difficulties into which his firſt Errors had plunged him.

His Conduct with regard to the *French* was to the full as inconſiderate, and no leſs inconſiſtent. His Kindneſs, Friendſhip, or whatever it was towards them, was as fatal as his Averſion or Diſlike had been to the *Engliſh*, and productive of the very ſame Misfortunes. He was undoubtedly impoſed upon and miſled by the falſe Impreſſions he received from them of their Strength: But in this he was inexcuſable, as theſe Repreſentations were grounded only upon vague and uncertain Reports of what they had done, and of what Strength they had in other Parts of the *Indies*, from whence all the Aſſiſtance they could give him was to be hoped, and this againſt a Power, the Weight of which he had already felt; and to ſay nothing of the Obligation he was under to maintain that Peace he had ſolemnly confirmed by his Oath, which was ſtill at his very Doors. If he had really intended, as he ſeemed very deſirous it ſhould be believed it was his Intention, to preſerve Peace in his Dominions, and to prevent the *Engliſh* and *French* from committing Hoſtilities againſt each other in them, to the Prejudice of Commerce, in which he was principally intereſted, and which was alſo, and was allowed to be, the common Concern of all, he might by acting firmly have carried that Point, by inſiſting upon a Neutrality under his Guaranty, and a peremptory Declaration that he would ſtop the Trade, and ſeize the Effects of that Nation, which violated a Neutrality ſo concluded; ſince under this it is certain the *Engliſh* would have acquieſced, and, without the Encouragement

or

or Aſſiſtance of the Suba, the *French* durſt not have broke it. But his Intrigues with them, or, as many thought, a Secret Treaty, encouraged their Director to declare, that he was not veſted with Authority to conclude any ſuch Neutrality; and even this, which he always knew, he did not acknowlege, until the Time was loſt, in which he might have obtained it from *Pondicherry*; and this plainly put the *Engliſh* under a Neceſſity of exerting the Force then in their Hands without Delay, which ended in the taking *Chandenagore*. Here again, if he had ever had any ſettled Principle of Action, would have been his Time to have ſhewn it; for if, upon Colonel *Clive*'s marching, he had aſſiſted the *French* with his whole Force, he might very probably have ſaved them. But as he had hitherto been all along the Dupe of their Politics, ſo in this Inſtance they were the Dupes of his, and were ſacrificed to his Want of Steadineſs and Spirit. On the whole, therefore, it became evident, that the Suba was more dangerous to his Friends than to his Enemies; and the Hazard of being hurt lay not in oppoſing, but in placing any Confidence in him. A Leſſon, which, as it had been

been taught by his firſt Actions, ſo, from the Bent of a ſtubborn Diſpoſition Events could not correct, he took care to inculcate it from time to time, as long as it was in his Power to act at all.

Colonel *Clive* uſed repeated Endeavours to extricate him, if he would have permitted it, out of all his Difficulties. He laboured in his Letters to convince him, that as the Attack and Reduction of *Chandenagore* proceeded entirely from the Behaviour of the *French* themſelves, ſo it could not be any-way prejudicial to him, or to his Subjects. He aſſured him, that the *Engliſh* would not ſuffer his Revenue to be impaired, by their being Maſters of the Place; but were diſpoſed, under equitable Conditions, to re-place the Cuſtoms paid by the *French*; and that they were well ſatisfied with their own Poſſeſſions, and did not deſire to enlarge or to extend them. On the contrary, they were ready to give him whatever Satisfaction he could demand, of their Willingneſs to acquieſce under any Terms, and to comply with ſuch Meaſures as ſhould appear moſt expedient for reſtoring and preſerving the Tranquility of his Country; that their

their Minds were entirely ſet upon Commerce; that they became military merely by Force; but that they moſt ardently wiſhed to return to, and be known by him only in, their old Occupation of Merchants; that, as things ſtood, their Intereſt rendered it abſolutely requiſite to expel the *French* out of *Bengal*, to prevent new Diſputes, which was his Intereſt likewiſe; and that, if he would do it himſelf, they ſhould be well ſatisfied, and conſider it as a Favour. That he had been exceedingly impoſed upon, in reſpect to the Conduct of that Nation, on the Coaſt of *Coromandel*, where the *Nabobs* they had eſpouſed were obliged to make exorbitant Grants, in Acknowlegement for their Aſſiſtance; that, in conſequence of this, they had torn away whole Provinces, of which they were in full Poſſeſſion; while, on the other hand, the *Engliſh* had lent the *Nabobs*, with whom they had taken Part, purely on account of their being the King's Officers, very large Sums of Money; with the Repayment of which they would be well content, without ſolliciting, extorting, or even accepting any Grants whatever. That he might from thence judge of the Temper of the two Nations, and the Difference that he would find in having either of them for his Allies; and that therefore, if he regarded his own Welfare, he would adhere ſtrictly to, and punctually fulfil, the Treaty he had made; which if he did, he might not only rely upon the Support that had been promiſed him, but that he might be aſſured, he would perſonally loſe the laſt Drop of his Blood, and ſacrifice the laſt Man under his Command, in his Service, againſt any of his real Enemies, whenever his Occaſions might require it. Vice-Admiral *Watſon* wrote alſo to him to the ſame Purpoſe.

The Suba, who was equally diſſatisfied with and diſturbed at the State of his Affairs, and found himſelf obliged to be at a great Expence in keeping Troops in the Field, knew not what to ſay or how to act. He declared, however, poſitively, againſt our reducing the *French* ſubordinate Factories; would not hear of making the Remains of their Forces Priſoners, and delivering them up to the *Engliſh*; but, however, diſcovered no Scruple at all in ſeizing upon their Effects, under Colour of doing it to make Satisfaction to his

own

own Subjects, who were their Creditors. At the ſame time he ordered the *French* to quit his Dominions, directing them to march towards *Patna*. He likewiſe paid farther Sums of Money to the Company's Servants, and gave them Hopes, that he would both ſtrictly and ſpeedily fulfil his Treaty in every reſpect. In regard to the Artillery, which he did not reſtore, he alleged, that he was diſtreſſed himſelf for want of Cannon, and was willing to purchaſe them. In this manner things went on for a Month or Six Weeks, during which Space every Method was practiſed that could leſſen his Apprehenſions, or free him from that Terror which he ſeemed to have of the *Engliſh* advancing their Forces into the Heart of his Country. He was even permitted, upon a Rumour that the Garriſon of *Caſſimbuzar* was augmented to Five hundred Men, to ſend his own Officers to inſpect it, who found and reported, that there was not above a Tenth Part of the Number. The ſame Compliances were made in many Reſpects.

But in the midſt of theſe Compliances and Conceſſions, inſtead of growing milder and better diſpoſed, the Suba ſhewed very evident Marks of his being more and more exaſperated againſt thoſe who gave them. He fell again to caballing with the *French*; and inſtead of compelling thoſe who had eſcaped to quit his Country, as he engaged expreſsly, he took that little Body of Men, which were about *Patna*, into his Pay, at the Rate of Ten thouſand Rupees a Month, of which Mr. *Watts* procured the Intelligence, and communicated it to the Committee. He turned all his Attention towards Mr. *Buſſy*, who, as he was made to believe, had an Army of Twenty thouſand Men, and with which he might march ſpeedily into his Dominions. When theſe Rumours at any time ſunk, he was more tractable; but as ſoon as they revived, he became as imperious and as much out of Humour as ever. Vice-Admiral *Watſon* having ſent him ſeveral preſſing Letters, exhorting him to act ſuitable to his Dignity, agreeable to his own Intereſts, for the Good of his Subjects, to give no Ear to idle Reports, to accompliſh his Promiſes, and fulfil the ſeveral Articles of his Treaty, he gave no Anſwers to them, but complained that they wrote in ſo ſevere a Stile, that he knew

not

not how to reply to them. At length his Uneasinesses, Jealousies, and Suspicions, rose so high, that he ordered all the Boats to be searched that came up to *Cassimbuzar*, and publickly declared, that if any Powder or Ammunition was found aboard, that he would order the Noses and Ears of the Watermen to be cut off, which was a direct Breach of his Treaty. He could not help knowing, that this Method of acting must have a very disadvantageous Effect upon the Affairs of the *English* in his Dominions, and impede and perplex their Commercial Transactions exceedingly. He could not be ignorant that this would diminish his own Income, distress his Subjects, and lessen both their Subsistence and their Industry. But alas! he was so much under the Dominion of his Passions, that he considered only gratifying his Caprice; and acting from no Motive, could discern no Consequences. Hapless as a Man! more hapless as a Prince! he had as little Fear of falling into Difficulties, as, when fallen, he had Skill to get out of them.

An Attempt has been already made to

give

give the Reader ſome Idea of the melancholy and mortifying Situation of Mr. *Watts*, who reſided on the Part of the Company at the Suba's Court, whoſe Perplexities daily increaſed, and whoſe Anxieties hourly multiplied, though they had not yet reached to thoſe Circumſtances of Diſguſt and Diſtreſs that they afterwards did. He ſaw himſelf almoſt conſtantly on bad Terms with that Prince, and of courſe upon no good ones with his Miniſters and Favourites. The Suba never forgave him extracting that important, and, as he conceived it, fatal Letter of Permiſſion to Admiral *Watſon*; to which, without much Injuſtice, he aſcribed ſolely the attacking and taking *Chandenagore*. It was from Mr. *Watts* he received, from Day to Day, thoſe grating Remonſtrances that ſo much diſpleaſed him, and thoſe admonitory Letters that made ſtill a deeper Impreſſion. He ought, in Strictneſs, to have conſidered him, on theſe Occaſions, as the Inſtrument only of the Company; but his Warmth and Aſſiduity in all theſe frequent Applications, made the Suba look no farther than himſelf. He was obliged to conſer with him daily, and, if he was abſent, called for him,

as

as being uneaſy if he miſſed him, whence of courſe he beheld him often, and yet but very ſeldom with a gracious Eye. Mr. *Watts* ſaw, felt, and underſtood theſe numberleſs Inconveniencies, to which he was expoſed, and which, as we have obſerved, heightened upon him every Hour. But the Conſolation he derived from the kind Letters of Admiral *Watſon* and Colonel *Clive*, who had a true and lively Senſe of his Services and Sufferings, kept up his Spirits, and enabled him to purſue his Buſineſs with a Vivacity that entirely concealed, though it could not remove, but rather augmented, his interior Chagrin. Beſides this, he had another Satisfaction, which was getting moſt Part of the Treaty executed, tho' with infinite Trouble; and this procured him the hearty Approbation of the Select Committee, who were now convinced, that he not only did all that could be done, but more than moſt Men could have done in his Station. As ill as he was treated by him, he continued to render the Suba many good Offices; giving the Committee to underſtand, that, in all human Probability, they ſhould gradually obtain all that they deſired, and that therefore they ſhould not be impatient.

He prevailed alſo upon Colonel *Clive* to promiſe the Suba from time to time his Aſſiſtance; and he laboured more inceſſantly to convince that Prince, that, if he would confide in the *Engliſh*, he had no Reaſon to fear either foreign or domeſtic Enemies, with which, when he thought himſelf in Danger, he was well enough pleaſed; but when that was in any Degree over, he ſhewed a viſible Uneaſineſs at his having confeſſed that he ſtood in need of ſuch Aſſiſtance.

The Storm, that had been gathering from the Beginning of *March*, began to burſt about the latter End of *April*, and in the Opening of the Month of *May*; when the Suba, in ſudden Starts of Paſſion, ſhewed the Rancour of his Heart, and teſtified ſufficiently, that he waited only for an Opportunity to make the *Engliſh* feel a ſecond Time the heavy Weight of his Reſentment. As he never aſſigned any Cauſes himſelf, but on the contrary, even in this Interval, and in the midſt of Actions inconſiſtent with thoſe Declarations, aſſerted his Intention to fulfil his Treaty, and appealed to God and his Prophet for the Truth of it; we muſt own it is extremely

extremely difficult to guefs at his Reafons. They appear, however, to have been chiefly Three; Firft, the perpetual Infinuations of the *French*, that Mr. *Buffy* might be brought to his Affiftance; and that, by a Junction with his Troops, he would be greatly fuperior to the *Englifh*; and to this Meafure he was fo much inclined, that he actually wrote a Letter to that Officer, in which he promifed him Twenty Lack of Rupees, if he would march directly into his Dominions, of which Mr. *Watts* alfo gave the Intelligence. The next Thing was, the Compliances that had been made with a View of gaining him, the recalling moft of the Troops from *Chandenagore*, the permitting him to keep the Cannon, to fearch the Factory of *Caffimbuzar*, and the warm and tender Expreffions of Friendfhip in Colonel *Clive*'s Letters, with the high Teftimonies of Reverence and Refpect paid him, whenever he was pleafed to be in a good Temper, or to profefs his Difpofition of adhering to his Engagements. The laft was, the Retreat of the *Patans*, who had fhewn an Intention to invade his Territories, and the putting an End to the Troubles occafioned by the *My Rajah*, by which he thought himſelf in a Condition to employ all his Forces, and was likewiſe ſecure of having the *French* to manage his Artillery, with which they made him believe they could perform Wonders. In theſe Circumſtances he was ſo very elate, as not to make any Scruple (though a direct Breach of his Faith) of interrupting the *Engliſh* Commerce, keeping his Army in the Field, though he had moſt ſolemnly promiſed the contrary, and ſometimes expreſſing a formal Deſign of ſending back the Treaty that had been ſigned with him, and demanding his own. In ſuch a State of Things it was evident, that the Company could not rely upon him, or conſider themſelves in any Degree of Security, farther than as they were ſupported by the King's Squadron and Forces; and as their preſent Condition was very precarious, ſo their future Proſpect was ſtill more gloomy and alarming; and though as yet they were not in a ſtate of War, they could not, however, with any Propriety, be ſaid to be in Peace.

The Vice-Admiral and Colonel *Clive* were exceedingly embarraſſed, and found it very difficult to judge what Meaſures they were

were to take. If they advanced their Forces, or reſumed their military Preparations, it might, in Appearance, juſtify the Suba's Behaviour; and beſides, Mr. *Watts* and the Select Committee both diſſuaded any Steps of this kind, as inconſiſtent with the Company's Concerns, at leaſt till they had ſecured the Money and Effects of the ſeveral Subordinates. On the other hand, they ſaw that Compliances did more Harm than Good, and that their Profeſſions of adhering inviolably to the Peace, and their repeated Promiſes of Friendſhip and Aſſiſtance, only flattered the Suba's Pride, heightened his Notions of his own Power, and encouraged him to act with greater Violence and Inſolence, of which they had but too many, and thoſe flagrant Inſtances. Colonel *Clive*, however, took on one Side every Method that was neceſſary to demonſtrate his pacific Inclination, and how ſincere his Intentions were to reſtore and preſerve the Tranquility of the Provinces, deſiſting from his Demands that the *French* ſhould be delivered up, from the repairing the Fortifications at *Caſſimbuzar*, or reinforcing the Garriſon. At the ſame time, he wrote in very plain Terms to the Suba, told him his Thoughts of his Proceedings, the Concern they gave him, and the Determination he had taken, to recur to open Force, whenever he found, from his Manner of acting, that no other Remedy was left, and that it was entirely in his Power to have him for a Friend or an Enemy. In the very Height of these Disputes, the Suba demanded an ample Acquittance, under the Seal of the Governor and Select Committee, and those also of the Vice-Admiral and Colonel. To this the latter wrote him for Answer, that it was strange he should demand, or expect such an Acquittance, when he very well knew, that several of the Articles were still unperformed; that many Lacks of Rupees were due to the Company, in Satisfaction of their Losses; that the Restitution of Thirty-eight Villages, which they claimed, had not yet been made; and that their Commerce in general was still interrupted. But as his Demand might imply a Resolution to settle all these Points, and as it was hoped this was really the Case, such an Acquittance should be immediately prepared, and transmitted to Mr.

Mr. *Watts*, with expreſs Orders to deliver it, as ſoon as the Articles hitherto unadjuſted were once thoroughly ſettled.

This, however reaſonable in itſelf, was by no means acceptable to the Suba, who, in Proportion as he loſt all ſeeming Regard, though really he never had any for the Vice-Admiral and the Colonel, towards both of whom he had once profeſſed ſo much Eſteem, kept no longer any Meaſures towards Mr. *Watts*, whom he looked upon as a Man he could not deceive, as a Man whom he hated for that Reaſon, and, which was an additional Motive to his Reſentment, though it ſhould, if his Mind had correſponded with his Rank, have reſtrained it, as a Man abſolutely in his Power. In order to execute the various Commiſſions with which he was charged more punctually, Mr. *Watts*, according to the Cuſtom of *Indoſtan*, had employed a Perſon to act as his Agent, in the Language of the Country, a *Vaqueel*. Him, in the firſt Fit of his Fury, the Suba forbid his Court. An Affront very groſs in *India*, though in Appearance, and to us, unacquainted with their Cuſtoms, a very ſlight Thing, but it was quickly followed by personal Insults, and those of the most serious Nature. At last, forgetting the Respect due to the *British* Crown, to Mr. *Watts*'s Character as Resident from the *East India* Company, and his own Dignity, he told several of his principal Ministers, with a View that they should, as they really did, tell it Mr. *Watts* again, that, upon the first Intelligence he had of the Motion of the *English* Troops, he would cut off that Gentleman's Head, or cause him to be impaled. This was such an Outrage on the Law of Nations as was inconsistent with the Rank of a Prince, and must, by the Rules of common Sense, leave any Man in his Circumstances at Liberty to take the Methods that appeared to him safest for his own Preservation. Upon this Occasion Mr. *Watts* acted with a Degree of Temper and Calmness that must surprize the Reader. He wrote an Account of the Facts to the Governor, without any Exaggeration, adding, that he despised the Suba's Threatenings, and desired the Select Committee would proceed as the Company's Interest directed, and without putting themselves in Pain for his Safety. A Circumstance that would not have been inserted in these Me-

moirs,

moirs, if the Perſon was not alive to whom that Letter was addreſſed.

The Gentlemen entruſted with the Direction of Affairs, ſaw plainly the Tendency of the Suba's Proceedings. Indeed they were ſo evident, as to fill all the Inhabitants of *Calcutta* with Alarms, that were but too well founded. Experience had already taught them, how far the Caprice of the Suba might go; and it was no way improbable, that if they were ſo unhappy as to fall again under his Power, they might, if poſſible, meet with ſtill worſe Treatment, which induced them to make the beſt Proviſion they could for their Defence; and to put the Troops into ſuch Condition, as that, whenever Neceſſity required, they might be able to repel Force by Force. At the ſame time, however, it was reſolved, not to precipitate any thing, to act with the utmoſt Caution, and to lay hold of any favourable Opportunity that might offer, towards furniſhing Means to extricate them from theſe Perplexities.

Calcutta was not the only Place where Doubts and Apprehenſions reigned. They

were

were to the full as ſtrong in *Muxadavad*, with this additional and diſtinguiſhing Circumſtance, that Diſcord ſpread itſelf through the Suba's Court, where the only Oracle that every Man conſulted was his own Intereſt. Reverſes of Fortune were equally ſudden and frequent. The Courtiers that were in the higheſt Favour To-day, were To-morrow in the very Depth of Diſgrace. No Man was ſecure, and therefore no Man was contented; and which is, and will be always the Caſe in corrupt Courts, the worſt Men had the beſt Chance. Thoſe who had nothing to loſe, had all Things to expect; and by flattering their Prince's Humour, and complying blindly with all his Commands, the meaneſt and baſeſt People about him grew quickly the moſt conſiderable. Thoſe who had been in the Old Suba's Councils and Confidence, who were Men of Rank and Family, and who had both Eſtates and Reputations to riſque, were, from thoſe very Circumſtances, Malecontents. They ſaw that this Syſtem could not laſt long; that a general Confuſion muſt enſue; and that a Man, governed entirely by his Paſſions, could never carry on public Affairs with any Degree of Succeſs. But theſe

Re-

Reflections, which their own good Senſe and long Experience ſuggeſted to them, ſerved only to diſturb and to diſtract, without afford-fording them the leaſt Glance of extricating either him or themſelves from that impending Ruin, which his raſh and raw Meaſures rendered inevitable. They perceived plainly enough each other's Sentiments, from that Tincture which they naturally gave to every One's Language and Behaviour; but they had no Confidence at all amongſt themſelves, and every Man was afraid of haſtening his own particular Fall, by diſcloſing or lamenting the Approach of that common Deſtruction, which, however viſible to their Underſtandings, was by no means a fit Subject for their Converſation.

But in the midſt of theſe Perplexities a Ray of Hope very unexpectedly appeared. The Suba had ſhewn the Severity of his Nature, in ſo many Inſtances, as to ſtrike a univerſal Terror; more eſpecially as the Fickleneſs of his Diſpoſition ſuffered no Man who was near him, and in his Power, to think himſelf ſafe. In ſuch a State of general Danger, there occured to every One, capable

pable of thinking freely (the only Species of Liberty that even Tyrants Favourites retain) but one ſingle Mode of Security, which conſiſted in depriving him of his Power, who ſo conſtantly, as well as egregiouſly abuſed it. The Conception of this availed little, ſince the Attempt was equally difficult and dangerous; and the failing in it ſure to be attended with ſudden and certain Deſtruction. There was alſo but one way to move, or rather to leſſen the Riſk; and this alſo was very eaſily diſcovered. It was procuring the Countenance and the Aſſiſtance of the *Engliſh*. Such as were in the Suba's Confidence, and from that very Circumſtance moſt afraid of him, were perſuaded they could merit very much from the Company's Servants, by laying open his Secrets, and thereby ſhewing them, what theſe People thought they did not in the leaſt ſuſpect, the Danger to which they ſtood expoſed. Amongſt ſeveral who reaſoned thus in their own Breaſts, there was one who had a conſiderable ſhare of Intereſt and Authority. His Name was *Godar Yar Cawn Laitty*, who, when he had for ſome time meditated, and in his own Mind thoroughly digeſted his Scheme, thought it wore

ſo

ſo fair an Appearance, that he ſent ſeveral Meſſages to Mr. *Watts*, ſignifying that he had ſomething to communicate to him of great Importance: But the Suba kept ſo many Spies upon that Gentleman, and thoſe Spies watched him ſo very cloſely, that it was ſimply impoſſible to comply with *Godar Yar Cawn Laitty*'s Requeſt of having an Interview with him, becauſe it was evidently riſking the utter Ruin of both. Some Days, therefore, elapſed, before an Expedient could be found to remove this troubleſome Obſtacle, and to give Mr. *Watts* the neceſſary Information of what were this Perſon's real Intentions, and what the Means by which he propoſed to carry them into Execution.

He at length thought proper to ſend to him *Omichund*, who has been mentioned before, in order to draw what Lights he could from this diſcontented Confident of the Suba, who, after he had conferred with him, reported, that he knew with Certainty his Maſter's ſettled Intentions were to break with and to attack the *Engliſh*, as ſoon as he had a favourable Opportunity; that he likewiſe knew the Suba had retained the *French*, who

had

had eſcaped from *Chandenagore*, and in the ſubordinate Factories, in his Service, who were to remain at *Patna* in his Pay, till an Occaſion could be found for employing them; that the *Engliſh* had no Method of preventing this threatening Tempeſt from breaking upon their Eſtabliſhments, but by providing in Time a Force ſufficient to reſiſt it; that he was willing, whenever the Suba ſhould recur to open Hoſtilities, to join Us, and act againſt him, provided we would aſſiſt him in aſſuming the Government of the Province; that in return for this, he would, as ſoon as he was fixed in that Office, grant, by way of Recompence, a large Extent of Lands to the Company, and would likewiſe pay down a Sum in ready Money, ſufficient to indemnify the People of *Calcutta* for all the Loſſes they had ſuſtained. Theſe were Communications of ſo dangerous as well as ſo delicate a Nature, that they would infallibly have turned a weak Head, or diſtracted a timid Mind. They were received calmly and coolly, as Points of Information, in regard to which Mr. *Watts* could take no Step of himſelf, but from which the Perſons who had communicated them had nothing to fear; and with theſe

these Aſſurances, ſuch was their Opinion of his Secrecy, Sagacity, and Steadineſs, that they remained perfectly ſatisfied and eaſy, leaving him ſufficient Leiſure to conſider and reflect upon theſe very extraordinary Overtures, and to review and digeſt the Thoughts that muſt naturally ariſe upon ſo important a Subject. But, however, reſtrained him within the Compaſs of Six Days, to procure for this *Mooriſh* Officer an Anſwer, from thoſe who were entruſted with the Management of the Company's Affairs at *Calcutta*.

The Situation of Mr. *Watts* in this Conjuncture, is much more eaſy to conceive than to deſcribe. He was oppreſſed with Cares, environed with Perils, and had not ſo much as a ſingle Perſon with whom to communicate or to conſult. His own Safety, the Welfare, and even the Being of the *Britiſh* Settlements, and indeed the future Fate of theſe Provinces, depended, at leaſt in the firſt Inſtance, on his Capacity, Penetration, and Diſcretion. It was a very arduous Taſk to form any clear Opinion upon this Offer; it demanded much Skill to ſet the Motives upon which ſuch an Opinion muſt be founded in their

their proper Light; and, when all this was done, it appeared infinitely hazardous to tranſmit Propoſitions of this Nature, together with his Thoughts upon them, to *Calcutta*, while a jealous Prince, in a Country where the Character of a Spy is not diſhonourable, had Multitudes of ſuch State Implements about him, all filled with the Hopes of riſing upon his Ruin. But though perfectly ſenſible of all this, as he muſt have been to counteract their Vigilance, he boldly undertook, and as happily performed, all that the Confidence repoſed in him, or his Duty to the Company could demand. He ſtated fully the Nature of theſe Overtures, the Suba's Diſpoſition at the Time, the Characters and Credit of the principal Officers about him, their Tempers, Circumſtances, and Connections, the Probability that ſuch a Deſign might be carried into Execution, the Hazards to which it muſt be expoſed, and the Methods moſt proper to avoid them. But when he had done all this, he added no direct Judgment of his own. He contented himſelf with giving Lights, without venturing to pronounce what Meaſure ought to be taken. He had frequent Experience of the Regard paid by them

them to his Sentiments, from his having commonly ſent them the Draughts of the Letters to the Suba, which being tranſmitted back to him, he preſented to that Prince; but he held this to be a Matter too difficult, as well as too delicate for him to determine. He knew very well there was no ſmall Danger in Delay; but he likewiſe knew, that there was ſtill more Danger in a raſh Deciſion, and therefore he gave none. The Select Committee concurred with him in this; they entertained the Motion, commended his Caution, ſuggeſted that he ſhould continue to keep Things in Suſpenſe, but directed him by all Means to avoid concluding any Thing, till he ſhould receive their future Directions in a Thing of ſo great Weight.

It was not long after this, that *Meer Jaſfeir Aly Cawn*, a Perſon of great Diſtinction, who had married the Siſter of *Aliverdy Cawn*, the Suba's Grandfather and Predeceſſor, ſent one in whom he could perfectly confide to Mr. *Watts*, to diſcloſe what were his real Opinions, and how very ſhort a Space he thought was like to intervene, before the Suba took the Field once more,

 againſt

against the *English*. This Person had it farther in Commission to represent, that the Disaffection of the principal Officers, Civil and Military, was in a manner general; that *Meer Jaffeir* never appeared in the Suba's Presence, without Fear of being assassinated; and that for this Reason, whenever he was constrained to go, he always caused his Forces to be drawn out, under Arms, with his Son at their Head. In the Close of his Discourse, he added, that a Determination was already taken, to depose, for their own Sakes, *Suraja Dowlat*; and that if the *English* would engage with, and promise to support, another Person, in assuming the Dignity of Suba, *Rahim Cawn*, *Roydoolub*, and *Bahadar Aly Cawn*, were ready to join *Meer Jaffeir*, in removing *Suraja Dowlat*, whose Affairs would be then in a very desperate Situation. Mr. *Watts* transmitted the Detail of this Conversation also to Colonel *Clive*, and gave it as his own Opinion, that *Meer Jaffeir* was by far the properest Person to be elevated to that Rank, as his Abilities were greater, his Reputation better, and his Connections more extensive than those of *Laitty*. He at the same time acquainted the Colonel, that if this Change

was

was to be accomplished by their Forces, as he much doubted, whether, after all, the *Moors* had Spirit enough to attempt so extraordinary an Enterprize themselves, it would be right to form the Outlines of a new Agreement, of which the old one ought to be the Basis; and to frame such additional Articles, as might effectually indemnify the Company for the Risk they ran, and procure an ample Satisfaction for the Losses private Persons had sustained, in the Devastation of *Calcutta*, of which no Care had been taken in the former Treaty; and that, in short, nothing should now be omitted, that might put their Affairs for the future upon a firm and stable Establishment; so that, in case of Disturbances in the Country, the Servants of the Company, and those who depended on it, might be in a Condition to protect themselves.

As these Transactions were of a very delicate Nature, and were to be conducted with much Discretion, and of course with some Delay, the Suba had a Season of Recess, in which, by a Change of Measures, he might have recovered his Authority, have resettled his distracted Government, and repaired all his past Errors. He not only neglected this entirely, but continued acting, in every respect, as if he had aimed at his own Destruction. He endeavoured to negotiate Succours from some of his Neighbours, who, though they knew not the Weakness of his Condition, and therefore civilly entertained his Proposals, had however such an Opinion of the Weakness of his Conduct, that nothing could induce them to enter into his Measures. He continued corresponding with Mr. *Bussy*, from whom he received Letters, which served to support and increase his Delusion, and to flatter him with the Hopes of seeing an Army of Twenty thousand Men in his Dominions, which, could he have brought them, would have tended only to have impoverished his Subjects, and to have given him new Masters, under the Title of old Allies. He was courted all this time by Colonel *Clive* to lay down his Arms, to settle the few reremaining unaccomplished Articles in the Treaty, and, above all, to put the Trade of his Territories into its usual Channel, for the common Benefit of the *Europeans* and the Natives. To these Sollicitations he gave

no

no Anſwers, or ſuch as afforded no ſort of Satisfaction; but, on the contrary, indicated very plainly, by every Step he took, that he meditated new Diſturbances, and waited for what ſhould appear to him a favourable Occaſion for renewing the War. In reference, on the other hand, to his own People, he grew every Day more and more intolerable, removing, diſgracing, inſulting, thoſe whom he had formerly treated with the greateſt Marks of Favour and Reſpect, and of whom ſeveral fled privately and in Diſguiſe to ſeek Shelter in the *Engliſh* Territories, and particularly in that of *Caſſimbuzar*. By this Behaviour he not only augmented the Diſaffection that had already ſpread ſo far amongſt his Servants, but likewiſe furniſhed ſo many and ſuch authentic Proofs of his having ſtill the ſame Points in View, that he had at his Entrance on the Adminiſtration, and of the Obſtinacy of his Averſion to the *Engliſh*, ſo contrary to the Mutability of his Temper in every thing elſe, that it contributed exceedingly to fortify the Sentiments of thoſe, who maintained, that the Peace of that Part of *India* could never be effectually reſtored, ſo long as he held the Supreme Power.

After the Propositions made by Mr. *Watts* had been duly canvassed, and their Importance maturely considered, by the Select Committee, who upon this Occasion framed and took an Oath of Secrecy, they were unanimously approved, and the Project or Draught of a new Treaty was transmitted to him. But at the same time there was great Latitude left, in case of Objections; and he was requested to procure as many and as large Concessions as might be, in case he found it impracticable to obtain every one of the Conditions in the full Extent that they desired. Indeed they relied so entirely upon him, that a Blank was left for the Company's Demand in their Draught of the Treaty for him to fill up; and how it was filled up, will appear from the Treaty itself. This was not only expedient but necessary, as he was upon the Spot, knew the Persons with whom he was treating, their Connections and Circumstances, and the Motives which might render any of these Demands agreeable or disagreeable. The use Mr. *Watts* made of this Confidence was such as it deserved, and turned not a little to the Advantage of those who gave it. He was himself perfectly fenfible, and took all imaginable Pains to make thofe he dealt with no lefs fenfible, that, notwithftanding this Change was for their mutual Benefit, yet the Weight, the Hazard, and the Expence, would fall principally at leaft, very probably wholly, upon the *Englifh*. He reprefented, therefore, effectually, that for fuch extraordinary Affiftance, which alone could put the Means of making it into their Power, a proper Satiffaction ought in Juftice to be made, and that this fuitable Satisfaction fhould be made likewife in a proper Manner. He was apprehenfive alfo, upon this Head, that a falfe Delicacy might produce future Difputes, and therefore very prudently provided, that the unliquidated Demands in the Sketch fhould be reduced to a Certainty. He alfo enlarged the Sums ftipulated for the Loffes of private Perfons, and diftinguifhed them under National Heads; that, if poffible, no Jealoufies or Heart-burnings might arife in the Colony, when they came to be actually paid.

The fureft as well as the fhorteft Method of fetting this Matter in a true Light, and that will at once place it in the ſtrongeſt, is to inſert the original Plan of the new Alliance, as tranſmitted to Mr. *Watts*, and then the Project ſettled by that Gentleman, which the Reader will hereafter have an Opportunity of comparing with the Alliance concluded.

Copy of the ARTICLES of Agreement ſent by Colonel *Clive* to *William Watts*, Eſq; *May* 2, 1757.

AN Alliance offenſive and defenſive againſt all Enemies: The *French* Fugitives to be taken and delivered up to us; all their Factories to be delivered up to us, in order to be deſtroyed; the *French* never to be permitted to re-ſettle in this Subaſhip; in Conſideration of which, the *Engliſh* Company will annually pay the Amount of Duties uſually paid into the King's Treaſury on the *French* Trade, or a Sum not exceeding Fifty thouſand Rupees annually.

Reſtitution of the Company's Loſs, by the taking of *Calcutta*, and their Out Settlements; alſo Reſtitution for the Loſſes of all *Europeans*

 by

by *Ditto*, as may be ſtated fairly by Admiral *Watſon*, the Governor, Colonel *Clive*, *William Watts*, Eſq; Major *Kilpatrick*, and Mr. *Becher*.

Blacks and *Armenians* are not included.

That the whole of our Phirmaund be complied with, and all other Grants made to us, particularly in the Treaty with *Suraja Dowlat*.

That the Bounds of *Calcutta* are to extend the whole Circle of *Ditchdug*, upon the Invaſion of the *Marattes*; alſo Six hundred Yards without it, for an Eſplanade.

The Inhabitants within our Bounds to be entirely ſubject to the *Engliſh* Laws and Government.

That we have Liberty to fortify and garriſon our Factories of *Caſſimbuzar* and *Dacca*, as we think proper, and a ſufficient Eſplanade be granted us round each.

That Convoys to and from one of our Settlements to another, be permitted to paſs without Interruption or Moleſtation.

That

That the *Moors* shall erect no Fortifications within Twenty Miles of the River Side, from *Hughley* to *Ingelee*.

That a Tract of Land be made over to the *English* Company, whose Revenues shall be sufficient to maintain a proper Force of *Europeans* and Seapoys, to keep out the *French*, and assist the Government against all Enemies.

That whenever the *English* Troops are called to the assistance of the Government, that the extraordinary Expences of the Campaign be made good by the Government.

That an *English* Gentleman, in Quality of Envoy, be permitted to reside at Court, and be treated with due Respect.

Minutes of the Treaty, by Mr. *Watts*, *May* 14, 1757.

I. That he will confirm all the Grants the former Nabob made us.

II. He will make an Alliance with the *English*, offensive and defensive, against all Enemies, either Natives or *Europeans*

III. What-

III. Whatever *French* are in his Provinces of *Bengal*, *Bahar*, or *Orixa*, to be delivered up with all their Houfes and Factories, and they never permitted to fettle more in either of thofe Provinces.

IV. On Account of the Company's Lofs * —— —— } 1 Crore.

* The Rupee is a Silver Coin, ftruck in the *Moghol's* Mints, with an Infcription of his Name and Titles, the Year of his Reign, and the Place at which it was ftruck. It weighs from 7 *dw.* 10 ⅓ *gr.* to 7 *dw.* 11 *gr.* and the Proportion of Allay to fine Silver, is as 1 or 2 to 100. One hundred thoufand Rupees make a Lack, One hundred Lacks a Coroe or Crore, One hundred Crores an Arrib.

TABLE of RUPEES.

Lack of Rupees.	£. *Sterling.*
1	12,500
10	125,000
20	250,000
30	375,000
40	500,000
50	625,000
60	750,000
70	875,000
80	1,000,000
90	1,125,000
Crore	1,250,000

V. On

V. On Account of the Losses of *Europeans* — — } 30 Lack.

VI. Ditto *Jentoows* — — 30 D°.

VII. Ditto *Armenians* — — 10 D°.

VIII. Ditto for *Omichund* — — 30 D°.

IX. Whatever Ground there is within the *Calcutta* Ditch, belonging to the *Zemindars*, to be given to the *English*, and Six hundred Yards without the Ditch all round.

X. A Tract of Land, whose Rents in the King's Books amounts to 100,000 Rupees Yearly, to be bought at a reasonable Value, from the Zemindary, and the Nabob to assist us in the Purchase, we paying the annual Piscash or Revenue, as usual, to the Nabob. Whatever Profit may arise from this Zemindary, is to go towards paying our Military.

XI. Whenever the Nabob wants the Assist-

ance

ance of our Troops, the extraordinary Expence to be paid by him.

His Plan of the Treaty was returned, with Alterations: Some of the Articles were modified, and a Blank left for the Company's Demand, that in caſe *Meer Jaffeir* ſhould think it too extravagant, Mr. *Watts* might have Liberty to moderate it, and he was deſired to get it carried into Execution; but it will appear in the Treaty itſelf, which will be hereafter given, that Mr. *Watts* got the Treaty executed, without any Deduction or Modification. This was a Work equally arduous and hazardous, as Things then ſtood, when every Look, every Word, every Motion of his was ſuſpected, and which at the ſame time rendered the procuring its Concluſion expeditiouſly a Circumſtance of the utmoſt Conſequence. In all this, the Riſk might be truly ſaid to fall entirely upon himſelf; ſo that it is not eaſy to imagine, how any Man's Circumſtances could be more critical than his actually were in this Conjuncture. We ſhall however ſee, that they really became ſo afterwards, and this in a very high Degree, and in very many Reſpects, from Cauſes that could

not

not be avoided, and which produced a Train of unforeseen Events.

It was pretty early known, that *Meer Jaffeir* had entertained no very favourable Notion of *Omichund*, but there was a Necessity of employing and trusting him notwithstanding, of which though the former did not complain, yet he did not dislike him the less. In the midst of these arduous Transactions, and when every one else had their Hands and their Hearts full, it came into *Omichund*'s Head to practise a little upon *Suraja Dowlat*, probably that he might be sure of somewhat, however Things went. He mentioned to Mr. *Watts* this very fine-spun Project, to which, that it appeared wild and strange, was by no means the strongest Objection. It was, however, in vain to make any: there was Money he thought to be got, and, if it was possible, he was resolved to get it. On the Sixteenth of *May* he went to the Palace, where, exerting his admirable Faculty of magnifying the Utility and exalting the Credit of the Advice he had to give, and having first alarmed the Suba's timid Mind, by touching many Subjects he knew

were

were diſagreeable, and in the Cloſe, when he ſaw him ſufficiently amazed, condeſcended to hint, that he had found means, with great Difficulty, to come at a Secret of the laſt Conſequence, and for the revealing of which he was ſure to loſe his Life, if it was ſo much as ſuſpected that he had penetrated and diſcloſed it. Promiſes of every kind were made, and at length out it came, that the *Engliſh* had diſcovered all his Negotiations with Mr. *Buſſy*, ſome Circumſtances of which he mentioned; that, upon this, they had ſent two Gentlemen to confer with, and to convince him, how much more it would be for his Intereſt to concur with them; and that they had made, or were upon the Point of making, a Peace; which, without doubt, muſt be at his Expence. As ſtrange as it may ſeem, *Omichund* prevailed over a Man's Foibles, which he had ſtudied, and deluded him into a firm Belief of all he ſaid, and, in conſequence of this, he procured a Perwannah, that is, an Order from the Suba to the Burdwan Rajah, one of his Officers, for the Payment of Four Lack of Rupees which he owed him, and the full Reſtitution of the remaining Part of the Money, and all the Goods,

Goods, of which he had been deſpoiled at *Calcutta*. This he took wonderful Care to have immediately executed, for fear of Accidents, that very Night; neither did he remain within the Suba's Reach long after. He left Traces, however, behind him, that ſufficiently juſtified *Meer Jaffeir*'s Suſpicions, and exerted that Power of perplexing, which he poſſeſſed in full as eminent a Degree as that of perſuading. This was one principal Cauſe of thoſe new Difficulties, to which Mr. *Watts* found himſelf expoſed, when he thought the whole Stock of his Abilities ſmall enough to deal with the old ones.

When the Agreement came to be offered to *Roydoolub*, one of the Suba's principal Miniſters, but, notwithſtanding that, one of the Parties to this Treaty, he made a Doubt as to the Poſſibility of complying with it. He ſaid, the Treaſury, ſince the Death of the Old Suba, *Aliverdy Cawn*, had been much drained, and that though *Suraja Dowlat* was indeed very rapacious, yet he managed his Affairs ſo ill, by keeping his Forces ſo long in the Field, as to have impoveriſhed himſelf by a vaſt, and at the ſame time uſeleſs Expence. He alſo ſuggeſted,

gested, that possibly in the Confusion that commonly attends every Revolution, the Suba's Treasury might be plundered, and then they should remain bound, without having it in their Power to pay. But to remove these Difficulties, he proposed it as an Expedient, to divide whatever was found in the Treasury with the *English*. Mr. *Watts*, who understood these People perfectly, consented to sign the Treaty with such a Clause, subject to the Approbation of the Select Committee at *Calcutta*. But when *Roydoolub* reflected, that upon such a Division he could pretend to no Commission, as he might on Money issued in virtue of the Treaty, of which he had Hopes given him; when Things came to a Crisis, he relinquished his own Proposal, and resolved to sign the Treaty as it stood. It appeared, that the Apprehensions which occasioned these Disputes, and this Delay, were insused into *Roydoolub* by *Omichund*, who gave him to understand, that if once the *English* Army took Possession of *Muxadavad*, they would not leave it again in three Years. This old crafty Man was not satisfied with giving this Proof of his Skill in embarrassing; he went much farther;

and as ſoon as he was himſelf out of Danger, divulged the Secret, which brought Mr. *Watts*, as well as *Meer Jaffeir* and the reſt, to the very Brink of Deſtruction; while at *Calcutta* he repreſented the whole Deſign as become deſperate and impracticable, becauſe it was diſcovered. It was, indeed, wonderful, all Things, and more eſpecially his Behaviour, conſidered, that it was not ſo. However, this Effect theſe Rumours had, that Confuſion increaſed, Diſcontent ſpread itſelf more and more in the Suba's Camp, and the Diviſions between him and his principal Officers grew daily wider and wider. *Meer Jaffeir* was fallen into open Diſgrace, removed from his Office of BUXY, or Paymaſter; upon which he withdrew, and continued in his Quarters with his Troops, and came no more near the Suba. A Circumſtance that rendered it next to impoſſible for Mr. *Watts*, who was ſenſible that he had many Spies upon his Conduct, to have an Interview with him, whoſe Houſe was entirely ſurrounded by the Nabob's Forces, without its being known; and this had given the Suba an Opportunity of executing his Threats, and if that had been a Thing he

regarded,

regarded, without much injuring his Reputation. The Matter, though ſo much embarraſſed, being ſtill abſolutely neceſſary, and the time preſſing, Mr. *Watts* went to him, in a covered Dooley, the Manner in which Women are conveyed in that Country, by which means he eſcaped Notice, and ſaw the Treaty which had been ſigned, ſealed, and ſworn to on the Koran, and upon his Son's Head, by *Meer Jaffeir*, with all the Solemnity imaginable, in the Evening of the Fifth of *June*. When this was once done, and authentic Advice received of its being done at *Calcutta*, it removed all Surmiſes, ſilenced every Suſpicion, and by giving entire Satisfaction, made way for the taking thoſe Meaſures which were requiſite for carrying it into Execution.

But before we proceed farther, it will be proper to look upon this Treaty, which with ſuch indefatigable Diligence Mr. *Watts* planned, proſecuted, and brought to bear, in deſpite of the Suſpicions, Spies, and inſidious Contrivances, of all his Enemies; by which the Company's Commerce, and all their Eſtabliſhments in this Part of *India*, were ſecured,

 the

the Losses which the Inhabitants of those Places had sustained, repaired, and the Honour of the Nation vindicated.

Translation of the TREATY made with *Meer Jaffeir.*

Wrote with his own Hand.

I Swear by God, and by the Prophet of God, to abide by the Terms of this Treaty, as long as I have Life.

Mir JAFFEIR KHAN BAHADAR,
Servant of King ALLUMGEER.

TREATY made with the Admiral, Colonel *Clive*, and the other Counsellors, Mr. *Drake* and Mr. *Watts.*

I. WHATEVER Articles were agreed upon in the time of Peace with the Nabob, *Suraja Dowlat*, *Munsurah Mimalek Shaik Kouli Khan Bahadar*, and *Hybut Jung*, I agree to comply with.

II. The

II. The Enemies of the *English* are my Enemies, whether they be *Indians* or *Europeans*.

III. All the Effects and Factories belonging to the *French*, in the Provinces of *Bengal*, *Bahar*, and *Orixa*, ſhall remain in the Poſſeſſion of the *English*; nor will I ever allow them to ſettle any more in the Three Provinces.

IV. In Conſideration of the Loſſes which the *English* Company have ſuſtained, by the Capture and Plunder of *Calcutta*, by the Nabob, and the Charges occaſioned by the Maintenance of their Forces, I give them One Coroe of Rupees.

V. For the Effects plundered from the *English* Inhabitants of *Calcutta*, I agree to give them Fifty Lack of Rupees.

VI. For the Effects plundered from the *Gentoows*, *Muſſulmen*, and other Subjects of *Calcutta*, Twenty Lack of Rupees ſhall be given.

VII. For the Effects plundered from the *Armenian* Inhabitants of *Calcutta*, I will give the Sum of Seven Lack of Rupees. The Distribution to be made of the Sums allotted the Natives, *English* Inhabitants, *Gentoows*, and *Mussulmen*, shall be left to the Admiral, Colonel *Clive*, *Roger Drake*, *William Watts*, *James Kilpatrick*, and *Richard Becher*, Esqrs. to be disposed of by them, to whom they think proper.

VIII. Within the Ditch, which surrounds the Borders of *Calcutta*, are Tracts of Lands belonging to several *Zemindars*, besides which, I will grant to the *English* Company Six hundred Yards without the Ditch.

IX. All the Lands lying to the South of *Calcutta*, as far as *Culpee*, shall be under the Zemindary of the *English* Company, and all the Officers of those Parts shall be under their Jurisdiction; the Revenues to be paid by them in the

the ſame Manner with other Zemindars.

X. Whenever I demand the Aſſiſtance of the *Engliſh*, I will be at the Charge of the Maintenance of their Troops.

XI. I will not erect any new Fortifications near the River *Ganges*, below *Hughley*.

XII. As ſoon as I am eſtabliſhed in the three Provinces, the Sums as aforeſaid ſhall be faithfully paid.

Dated the 15th *Ramzan*, in the Fourth Year of the preſent Reign.

The perfect Harmony that ſubſiſted between Vice-Admiral *Watſon* and Colonel *Clive*, and the intire Confidence repoſed in them by the Select Committee, was upon this Occaſion, as it had been often before, the principal Source of that Alacrity, with which every thing was undertaken. A Train was immediately provided, a Detachment of Fifty Sailors, with a full Compliment of Officers, appointed to aſſiſt thoſe who had the Direction of it; and Inſtructions were given for ſtationing a Twenty Gun Ship above *Hughley*, to keep the Communication with the Army open. Theſe Steps were abſolutely requiſite, and others of a like Nature were prudently contrived, and chearfully performed, by the Officers in the King's and in the Company's Service; the Select Committee did their Buſineſs in Silence; and though there was a warm Spirit of Emulation, yet the leaſt Spark of Envy or Jealouſy never appeared, though ſo many Corps of different Kinds were ſerving conjunctly in the Expedition. This, as it was truly ſingular, was alſo remarkably happy; for no Exploit of this Conſequence was ever begun or proſecuted in a more critical Situation, or where any untoward Accident might have more eaſily occaſioned a Diſappointment. The Forces that were to be employed, tho' more numerous than in the preceding Operations, yet were but a Handful, in compariſon of the Suba's Army. *Meer Jaffeir*, who had ſeparated his Corps of Troops, was again joined with the Suba, but without any real Reconciliation on either Part: Yet this, however, was ſufficient to raiſe a Doubt, how far any Dependance could be formed upon his acting; and what followed, plainly ſhewed

that

that Suſpicion was not ill founded. There was no ſmall Danger of being ſurrounded by theſe ſuperior Troops, and if the Communication with the River had been intercepted, the greateſt Difficulties might have enſued. Beſides theſe, the rainy Seaſon was juſt coming on; ſo that, all Things taken together, and the Hazard that was to be run being maturely weighed, the *Moors* embarked in this Deſign had not the ſmalleſt Reaſon to repine at the Price they paid for our Aſſiſtance; as on the other hand, their own Safety, and the large Stake for which they fought, being conſidered, the *Engliſh* had great Encouragement to exert themſelves with that ſteady Intrepidity which they did. Mr. *Watts*, from what he knew of the Suba's natural Diſpoſition, and what he had obſerved with reſpect to his Forces, and thoſe who commanded them, formed ſo true a Judgment of all that might happen, and had previouſly acquainted the Select Committee with theſe Sentiments, that there ſcarce fell out any Thing in the Progreſs of this Expedition which was not foreſeen, and in regard to which therefore the proper Precautions had not been taken.

After

After finiſhing his Negotiations with *Meer Jaffeir*, and taking all the Meaſures requiſite for executing his intended declining from the Suba in time of Action, and, if a favourable Opportunity offered, ſeizing his Perſon, there ſeemed to be no farther Neceſſity for Mr. *Watts* to continue under the Eye of a provoked and capricious Prince. But this very Circumſtance rendered it expedient; to diſtract his Thoughts, to give him a Diffidence of the Informations he received, and to afford Leiſure for the Preparations making at *Calcutta*. His Houſe was ſurrounded with Spies, who watched not only his Motions, but his Words and Looks. It may be, the ſtrong Aſſurances they gave, that he could take no Method to withdraw, but they muſt have previous Intelligence, contributed to his Safety. However, his Condition was moſt unhappy; a ſudden ſtart of Paſſion in the Suba had in a Moment brought him to a violent Death, at leaſt; perhaps, to Tortures. At *Calcutta* they had ſo true a Senſe of his Danger, that it was more than once reported, *Suraja Dowlat* had cut off his Head, and ſet it upon a Pole. There was likewiſe Doubts as to the Means of his eſcaping. He choſe

to

to do it with the reſt of the Gentlemen on Horſeback, the Manner leaſt ſuſpected, becauſe of the Length of the Journey, and the extreme Heat of the Seaſon, which rendered it exceſſively fatiguing, and not a little dangerous. But when he underſtood from Colonel *Clive*, that every thing reſpecting the Expedition was completed, he happily deceived the Spies of the Suba, and on the Eleventh of *June* made his Eſcape, though not unpurſued. It was not to *Calcutta* he directed his Courſe, but to the Army, in which he continued, and was preſent at the deciſive Action which brought on the Completion of his Treaty, and thereby reſtored Peace to *Bengal*. Let us now reſume the Operations of the *Britiſh* Forces.

All things being in Readineſs, the Army, which conſiſted of One thouſand *Europeans*, Two thouſand Seapoys, Fifty Seamen, under the Command of a Lieutenant, with Seven Midſhipmen, and Eight Pieces of Cannon, began their March from *Chandenagore* towards *Caſſimbuzar* on the 13th of *June*. The very ſame Day Mr. *Watts* joined the Colonel, to whom he imparted all the Lights,

Lights, and gave the best Intelligence in every Reſpect that was in his Power. On the Nineteenth the Town and Fort of *Cutwa*, ſituated on the ſame Side with *Chandenagore*, of that River which forms the Iſland of *Caſſimbuzar*, was attacked and taken. This was an Event of ſome Importance, as it opened a free Paſſage, which could not have been eaſily forced, if it had been properly defended. The Army halted there for two Days, in order to receive ſome Accounts of the Enemies Strength, as well as to gain certain Advice of what might be expected from thoſe who were entered into the Party with, and engaged to ſupport, *Meer Jaffeir*; which, when it arrived, was far enough from being ſatisfactory or explicit. The Colonel, however, was ſo well informed by Mr. *Watts*, as to the real Cauſes of this ſeeming Backwardneſs, and had from his own Experience and Penetration ſo juſt a Notion of the *Moors* Mode of acting, which, without ſuch previous Acquaintance with their Temper and Manners, might probably have confounded any other Officer in his Station, that on the Twenty-ſecond of the ſame Month he paſſed the River, and continued his March directly towards

wards *Plaiſſy*, where the Army arrived, and took up their Ground about One the next Morning, without meeting with any Diſturbance or Moleſtation on their March.

This Poſt was extremely well choſen for that Country, and for the Method in which thoſe People make War. It was a Grove, covered on every Side by Mud Banks, in the midſt of a Plain. At Day-break, on the Twenty-third, the Suba's Army advanced within a very ſmall Diſtance, and with a manifeſt Deſign to attack the *Engliſh* Forces. He had about Fifteen thouſand Horſe, and between Twenty and Thirty thouſand Foot, with upwards of Forty Pieces of heavy Cannon, which were managed by *Frenchmen*, upon whoſe Skill and Courage he greatly depended. The Van was commanded by *Roydoolub*, and and the left Wing by *Meer Jaffeir*. About Six they began to cannonade pretty ſmartly on every Side, and this Diſtribution of their Cannon gave them two great Advantages; Firſt, as they were much larger, and carried a heavier Weight of Metal, they did Execution where the *Engliſh* Artillery was of no Uſe; and in the next Place, being thus ſeparated

rated to a considerable Distance from each other, it was impossible to make any Attempt to seize them, and therefore all the Colonel could do was to take the Benefit of his intrenched Posts, and leave his Troops as little exposed as possible. If the Suba, or any of his Officers, had understood well what they were about, they might certainly have prosecuted their Scheme, and have completely invested the *English* Army, and then the Colonel must have waited the Approach of Night, in order to have forced a Passage through the Camp, which he in reality had designed. But the Enemy, on the contrary, upon the falling of a smart Shower about Noon, withdrew their Artillery within their Camp. Upon this, a Detachment marched with Two Field Pieces, and took Possession of a Tank, covered with high Banks, from whence the *Moors* had fired with Success. They then would have brought out their Artillery again, but were prevented; and this encouraged the sending Detachments to possess two other Eminences, very near an Angle of their Camp, covered by a double Breastwork; and from thence, as well as from another Eminence, which still remained in their

their Poſſeſſion, they kept up a pretty ſmart Fire with their Small Arms. They ſeveral times endeavoured to bring up Cannon to thoſe Poſts, but our Field Pieces were ſo happily poſted, and ſo well ſerved, that they could never effect it. At length the *Engliſh* ſtormed that Angle and Eminence at the ſame Inſtant of time, though the former was defended by Forty *French*, and a very numerous Body of the Suba's Troops, who had likewiſe in that Poſt Two Pieces of Cannon, and the latter by a conſiderable Corps of Foot and Horſe. Some Perſons of Diſtinction being killed immediately before, or at the Beginning of the Attack, the Enemy being diſpirited by that, quickly gave way, and both the Poſts were forced with a very trifling Expence to us, though they ſuffered ſeverely. On this the right Wing and Center fled, abandoning their Camp and Artillery. Their Loſs in this Action fell little, if at all, ſhort of Five hundred Men, and between Forty and Fifty Pieces of Cannon. Of the *Engliſh* Forces, there were Twenty killed and Fifty wounded, the greateſt Part of which were Seapoys. The Flight of the Enemy was ſo precipitate, that the Suba, mounted on a Camel, with the better Part of the Army, arrived at *Muxadavad*, which was Twenty Miles diſtant, by Twelve at Night. The Colonel, after purſuing them Five or Six Miles, halted his Troops; and diſpoſed of them in the beſt Manner he could. Such was the Battle, ſuch the deciſive Victory of *Plaiſſy!*

It was obſerved during the Action, that a great Body of Horſe, in the Enemy's left Wing, kept moſtly hovering at a Diſtance. But as they made no Signals; though they ſometimes advanced within Cannon-ſhot, they were more than once taught by our Artillery to retire. However, after the Victory was declared, the Colonel was informed that theſe were *Meer Jaffeir*'s Troops, which remained on the Field in a Body, and the next Day, in the Morning, he had an Interview with Mr. *Clive*, in which, after congratulating him upon his Victory, and applauding his Conduct, he ſignified his Willingneſs to ratify the Treaty, and to perform all the Articles of it punctually, as ſoon as it was in his Power. Colonel *Clive* adviſed him to march without Delay, and make himſelf Maſter of the Capital of the Provinces, before *Suraja Dowlat* could

could have Time to recollect himſelf, or draw together any conſiderable Part of his diſperſed Army. *Meer Jaffeir* ſaw the Utility of this Advice, which he carried into Execution with the utmoſt Expedition. At his Entrance into *Muxadavad*, he found the City in the utmoſt Conſternation. The Suba was in Poſſeſſion of his Palace, on the other Side of the River, with ſome Troops about him, amongſt whom he diſtributed ſeveral Lack of Rupees; but the reſt, as had been foreſeen, diſperſed. A few Hours after, in a Fit of Deſpair, he withdrew, accompanied only by Five Perſons, and took with him a large Sum in Gold, and Jewels to an immenſe Value. Upon the News of this, *Meer Jaffeir* immediately paſſed the River, entered the Palace, and aſſumed the Title of Suba, without any Oppoſition. At the ſame time, he ſeized the Treaſures of his Predeceſſor; and Things being in this Situation, he diſpatched Advice inſtantly to Colonel *Clive*. As there was ſtill a great Fermentation amongſt the People, and no Certainty of what was become of *Suraja Dowlat*, it was judged expedient, upon the Arrival of this News, to ſend Mr. *Watts* and Mr. *Walſh* thither, that they might uſe their beſt Endeavours to quiet the Metropolis, to fortify the new Suba, in his Diſpoſition to fulfil the Agreement, and to put an End to the preſent Confuſions, as ſoon as it was poſſible. They were fortunate enough to ſucceed in this important Commiſſion; and all things being reduced to a greater Degree of Order and Tranquility than could well be expected, Colonel *Clive* was invited to pay a Viſit to the Nabob. On the Twenty-ninth of *June* he made his public Entry into *Muxadavad*, attended by a Guard of Two hundred *Europeans*, and Three hundred Seapoys. He was received there with the utmoſt Expreſſions of Joy, and the loudeſt Acclamations of the People, as well as with the moſt profound Marks of Reſpect, and the warmeſt Teſtimonies of Gratitude, by *Meer Jaffeir*, with whom he went to the Palace; and ſaw him ſeated in Form, upon the MUSNUD, or Carpet of State, where he was unanimouſly ſaluted Suba, and thereby inveſted with the ſupreme Authority over the Provinces, with general Applauſe. Thus, in a Fortnight's Time, this amazing Revolution was begun and ended, and that happy Change effected, from which ſuch numerous Benefits have

have ſince flowed to the *Eaſt India* Company, and the *Britiſh* Subjects in *Bengal*.

About the ſame time the unfortunate *Suraja Dowlat* was ſeized, near *Rajamaal*: It is certain that he was in a very low and diſtreſſed Condition, with hardly any Cloaths upon his Back, and the Report went, that he ſought Shelter in the Houſe of a Man, whoſe Ears he had cauſed to be cut off in one of his Tranſports of Paſſion, and by whom he was diſcovered, and given up to his Purſuers. Be that as it will, the making him Priſoner was regarded as an Event of great Conſequence to the new Suba. He was no ſooner informed of it, than he committed that Prince to the Cuſtody of his Son, recommending to him earneſtly in public, to take the ſureſt Methods to prevent his Eſcape; but at all Events to preſerve his Life. The young Man, inſtead of paying that Reſpect which was due to his Father's Commands, no ſooner had him in his Hands, than he cauſed him to be privately put to Death. At this, when the Suba appeared to be diſpleaſed, his Son alleged, that the captive Suba had found means to write and convey Letters upon the Road to ſeveral

Jemidars, in order excite a Revolt in the Army; to prevent which, he knew no other certain Remedy than that of depriving him of Life, which he thought was likewiſe better done, without expecting any farther Orders. It has been ſurmiſed, and very probably not altogether without Grounds, that there was ſomething of Colluſion in this Matter between the Father and the Son; a thing indeed not at all unfrequent in this Part of the World; and what made it paſs for a kind of Juſtice, was the Remembrance that People had, that this unhappy young Man, *Suraja Dowlat*, had been often employed in the very ſame Acts, by the old Suba, *Aliverdy Cawn*, who availing himſelf of the ſanguinary Diſpoſition of his Grandſon, made uſe of him to remove ſuch as through Avarice, Suſpicion, or Reſentment, he inclined to have taken away, and then, to ſave Appearances, diſavowed the Fact.

Such was the End of *Suraja Dowlat*, in the Prime of his Youth, being at the Hour of his Death ſcarce Twenty-five Years of Age. An End! ſuitable to his Life, which had been ſpent in Violence and Blood. He was naturally

turally raſh and headſtrong, conceived the ſtrongeſt Reſentment on the ſlighteſt Occaſions, often without any Occaſion at all; and notwithſtanding the Variableneſs of his Nature, and the continual Fluctuation of his Mind, either executed ſuddenly the Dictates of his Paſſion, or, where that was impracticable, perſiſted in his bad Intentions, though he never ſhewed any Steadineſs in the Performance of his Promiſes, or any Regard to his Oaths, which he made and broke with the very ſame Facility. The only Excuſe that can be offered for him, is, that he had a View of Sovereignty from his Infancy; little, and that but bad, Education in his Youth; and, after all, lived not long enough to attain any great Experience, which poſſibly might have made him better, and poſſibly alſo might have made him worſe. His Reign was but of Fourteen Months, and in that Space he had little Quiet himſelf, allowed none to his Subjects; and with boundleſs Authority, and immenſe Riches, never excited Duty, or ſo much as acquired a ſingle Friend, whoſe ſage Advices might have prevented his ſad Cataſtrophe. How inſignificant then is Power! How deſtructive is Wealth! when they fall into the

Hands of him, who only poſſeſſes that he may abuſe them!

There was a Circumſtance attending the Fate of *Suraja Dowlat*, that perhaps contributed to make even the Manner of it leſs regretted. Mr. *Law*, who had been formerly the *French* Chief at *Caſſimbuzar*, a Gentleman, to do him Juſtice, of Honour and Abilities, had collected Two hundred of his Nation for the Service of the Suba, and was within a few Hours March of him when he was taken; upon hearing of which he ſtopped. This is a concluſive Proof that he was in his Pay, and a Circumſtance that very fully juſtifies the *Engliſh* in their Conduct. If he had reached, and preſerved *Suraja Dowlat*, the War would not have been ſo eaſily and ſo ſpeedily finiſhed. He who was without Friends in his Diſtreſs, might have again found Troops for Pay, or perhaps for Promiſes, ſo that his Death in this Reſpect had a ſtronger Air of Policy, and contributed to add Credit to the Report, that his Succeſſor was not ſo entire a Stranger to it as he ſeemed. This Event likewiſe made it evident, that the Article which provided againſt the Return

Return of the *French* into *Bengal*, was not either improper or imprudent. Colonel *Clive*, who sees Things and their Consequences in an Instant, detached Captain *Coote*, then of Colonel *Aldercron*'s Regiment, with Two hundred *Europeans*, and Five hundred Seapoys, in Pursuit of Mr. *Law*; and though that Force was fully sufficient, yet he engaged the Suba to send also Two thousand of his Horse, that his own Subjects and all *India* might know, that the *French* were equally his Enemies and Our's, and that being accustomed, from his first Entrance on Government, to fulfil his Engagements, he might learn to place his own Grandeur in adhering to his Word, and expect the Safety of his Dominions from the punctual Performance of his Promises. A Lesson that could not be taught at a more convenient Time.

The setting up the new, or rather restoring the old Form of Rule, was entirely due to the *English*, and the Suba and his Subjects were alike sensible of it; which was a Point of equal Honour and Advantage to the Nation. It afforded a strong and glorious Proof, that we, who in so long a Course of

Years had never given the leaſt Trouble or Uneaſineſs to the Government, were yet able to do ourſelves Juſtice, when there was no other way left to remain in Quiet. On the other Hand, all the Advantages gained were by the fair and open Method of a Treaty, in which the firſt and moſt difficult Part was performed by us, and not taken violently or by force of Arms; though at the ſame time it was evidently in our Power to have done it, if it had been at all in our Will. When, therefore, Colonel *Clive* and Mr. *Watts* applied themſelves to the Suba, for the ſpecific Performance of that Agreement, which he had made previous to his Acceſſion, the Juſtice of their Demand was without Heſitation acknowleged. The State of the Treaſury was laid before them in the moſt candid Manner, ſo as to leave them not the leaſt Reaſon to doubt, that what *Roydoolub* mentioned as an Objection at the concluding of the Treaty, was a real matter of Fact; and from the Diſſipation that had happened ſince, the Suba was not in a Condition to fulfil his Promiſes, and diſcharge all his Obligations at once. Beſides, it was for the Intereſt of the *Engliſh*, as well as for the Reputation of the Com-

Company, to ſupport the Government which had been the Work of their own Hands, and not leave a Prince whom they had raiſed to the Subaſhip, with a Treaſury abſolutely empty, ſince ſuppoſing this in their Power, it muſt have exceedingly diſtreſſed him, and no leſs diſgraced them.

In this State of Things, the Propoſition he made ſeemed too equitable to be rejected. He offered to pay down a third of the whole Sum, to make it up one Moiety in a very ſhort Space of Time, and to diſcharge the Remainder by equal Payments, in the Space of Three Years. This, therefore, was accepted, from a moral Perſuaſion that he, who parted with one Half in Conſideration of what had been done for him, would likewiſe pay the other Half in the limited Time, to ſecure Aſſiſtance, in caſe any thing more was to be done. Theſe then were the real Motives to the Agreement, which indeed took its Riſe from Neceſſity, a Law that maintains its Rights under every Government, and in all Climates. There is a known Cuſtom throughout *India*, and in that Country more than in any other Cuſtom has the Force of a Law, that

that Ten *per Cent.* is paid as Treaſury Fees upon all Sums received, which thoſe Gentlemen had Weight enough with *Roydoolub* to reduce to Five; and by the Help of this Conceſſion, every thing was very ſoon adjuſted, and the complete Moiety came into the Company's Poſſeſſion. The candid Reader will probably think that Colonel *Clive* and Mr. *Watts* did, upon this very momentous Occaſion, all that it was in their Power to do, and this was alſo their Sentiment; for as ſoon as more was in their Power, they took care to improve the Opportunity for the common Benefit of all concerned. A concluſive Teſtimony of the Uprightneſs of their Intention, in the whole of this Tranſaction.

This wonderful Sunſhine of Proſperity at *Calcutta* was ſuddenly overcaſt, by the Death of a Great Man, to whoſe Virtues and Abilities the Inhabitants were indebted, in a very high Degree, for all the Happineſs they poſſeſſed This was *Charles Watſon*, Eſq; Vice-Admiral of the Blue, whoſe amiable Qualities in private Life added Luſtre to his public Character. His Sentiments were noble, generous, and humane, his Manners graceful,

easy,

easy, and polite; no Gentleman was ever more capable of gaining the Esteem of those with whom he conversed, and no Officer ever understood better how to exercise the Benevolence and Sweetness of his own Disposition, without impairing his Authority. In his Station he was Active without Hurry; Vigilant, without seeming to be Busy; and, with an open Countenance, ever attentive to his Duty. His Orders were obeyed with Pleasure, because they were enforced by his Example; and he was himself ready to do more than he ever expected from others. His having the Command in that critical Conjuncture, was, from the Beginning, looked upon as a singular and signal Blessing to the *English* settled in the *Indies*; and every Action of his afterwards confirmed that Notion. No Wonder, then, that his Death was considered as a common Calamity, and his Loss regretted as a public Misfortune. He was interred on the Seventeenth of *August*, when an unfeigned Sorrow was plainly visible in the Face of every Inhabitant, and a voluntary universal Mourning expressed, in some Degree, the true Sense the People had of his Merit, and the Effects that had been derived to them from thence. Indeed, they had been inconſolable, but for the Hopes they had ſtill left in Admiral *Pocock*. Hopes! that did not deceive them, and which have been productive of new Honours to the *Britiſh* Flag.

It was to the Attention of the Adminiſtration at Home, that the Company and the Subjects of *Great Britain* in *India* owed theſe potent and timely Succours; and, which was of no leſs Conſequence, the prudent and happy Choice of the Officers who commanded them. The *French*, though deficient elſewhere, had a conſiderable Naval Force in the *Indies*, and were for this Reaſon very confident of their Succeſs in that Part of the World; in which, perhaps, they had not been deceived, if, upon the Demiſe of Vice-Admiral *Watſon*, the Command had devolved upon an Officer of leſs Merit, or even upon an Officer whoſe Merit had been leſs known or leſs eſtabliſhed than that of Mr. *Pocock*. As it was, the Spirits of *Britiſh* Subjects were not depreſſed, or thoſe of the Enemy raiſed. They had already known and felt his Courage, and he made them very quickly ſenſible of the Extent of his Capacity. They ſaw him

him equally active and vigilant: Their Squadrons no sooner appeared, than they had his in View. He was the Guardian of all our Settlements, and the Bane of all their Armaments and Expeditions. His Sagacity defeated many of their Designs, his Dexterity and Dispatch disconcerted others, till, by his Victories, he ruined, not their Reputation only, but their Strength in *Asia*, as completely as other Admirals had done in *Europe* and *America*. These are Facts indisputable; and, as they are connected with our Subject, we may take the Liberty of mentioning them, without giving Offence to that Gentleman, whose Modesty renders him as amiable, as his other Virtues have made him conspicuous. But to return to our Subject.

All Infant Governments are in their very Nature subject to Disorders. The new Suba, soon after the Departure of Colonel *Clive*, felt sufficiently, that, contrary to the first flattering Appearances, his Administration was not thoroughly established. Some of the Nabobs in his Province, dubious of his Intentions towards them, made no great haste to acknowlege an Authority that might be prejudicial

judicial to their own; and in the *Indies*, this kind of Delay is ever considered as Disobedience. Besides, *Meer Jaffeir* remembred the Advice which the Colonel had given him at Parting, which was, to acquire a Reputation for Firmness from his earliest Actions, if he meant to taste Quiet in the remaining Part of his Reign. He resolved, therefore, to employ his Forces against those, who, though they did not presume to question his Title, shewed, notwithstanding, a Reluctancy to acknowlege it. He found, however, a sudden Stop put to his Operations. At the Beginning, some of his Officers were intractable, and his Troops in general were unwilling to move. He was entitled by the Treaty to Assistance from the *English*, and, upon his making the Demand, Colonel *Clive* marched instantly to his Relief. His Forces were not numerous; but he brought with him a Reputation that carried with it a Persuasion that he was ever irresistable, and his very Presence in the Suba's Camp restored Obedience to that Prince. Colonel *Clive*, and Mr. *Watts* who attended him, took this Opportunity to sollicit the assigning Funds for the Money that was still due, and obtained from

from the Suba, though not without some Difficulty, all that they desired.

They likewise desired, and obtained, that the Company's Grant of Lands might be extended Northward from *Culpee* to *Rangafullah*, which, besides the Augmentation of Territory, was in other Respects a Matter of Importance.

The Nabob of *Patna*, whose Name was *Ramnaram*, against whom this Expedition was made, upon the Approach of the Suba's Army, offered to submit, and to pay his Tribute regularly, if he was continued in his Government, and the Suba's Promise was guarantied by Colonel *Clive*. The Suba requested this as a Favour of the Colonel, and desired that he would write a Letter to the Nabob, which he accordingly did; and upon the Faith of that Letter, he came and made his Submission. The great Product of *Patna* is Salt-petre, about which there had been formerly continual Disputes between us and the *Dutch*. At present, it was in the Hands of neither; but was still a Monopoly under a Lease. Colonel *Clive* and Mr. *Watts*,

4 who

who knew the Conſequence of ſuch an Acquiſition to the *Engliſh*, propoſed the giving it in Leaſe to them, at the ſame Rate, which would be no Prejudice to the Suba; and the Juncture being favourable, this Propoſition was complied with likewiſe, by which the Company are annually Gainers of about Two Lack and a half of Rupees, or ſomething more than Thirty thouſand Pounds Sterling. It is evident, therefore, from theſe Inſtances, that no favourable Opportunity was let ſlip, no ſingle Occaſion loſt, that could be turned to the Company's Advantage.

This Expedition, as it effectually fixed the new Suba in that Dignity, naturally brings the Memoirs of this Revolution to their Period. We cannot, however, conclude without obſerving, that as there could not be any thing more melancholy than the Situation of the Company's Affairs, when the Settlement of *Calcutta* was overwhelmed and deſtroyed, ſo nothing can be more ſatisfactory than to contemplate the Advantages that have reſulted from this Alteration to the *Eaſt India* Company, the private and particular Sufferers, and the *Britiſh* Subjects who either reſide

reside in, or may hereafter go and reside in, *Bengal*. In reference to the Company, the Treaty with the present Suba procured them an ample Indemnity, without tying them down to a Specification of Losses, which would have been not more impossible than improper. The Sum was such as became the Rank and Grandeur of him who gave, and was admirably suited to the Situation and Services of those who received. The Point of Security is likewise fully provided for; the Settlement may be fortified in such a Manner as to remove all Apprehensions; at the same time that these mighty Concessions are made, they are made in a Method that renders them doubly valuable, not through Fear or Compulsion, but with all possible Marks of Confidence and Esteem. The Interests of the Company, and the Country Government, are declared to be the same; and to prevent any Suspicion of Alteration, they are allowed an unrivalled Superiority, and the Enemies of the one are to be of Course the Enemies of the other. There is a Provision, as far as such a Provision can be made, that this Conjunction of Interests shall not be temporary, but perpetual; since the

Company is at Liberty to take whatever Meaſures ſhall ſeem moſt expedient for the Safety of her Settlements, which is as much as could be either expected or deſired.

The Regard ſhewn, and the Proviſion made, for all Degrees of Perſons, who ſuffered by the Subverſion of the Colony, was equally equitable and honourable. The Company, and thoſe who depended upon it, ſhared the good as well as the ill Fortune that attended the different Adminiſtrations in *Bengal.* There were many of the *European* Sufferers, who were abſolutely ruined and undone; reduced from Opulence and Eaſe, to Miſery and Want, by a ſudden, unforeſeen, and inevitable Misfortune. Theſe were reſtored to the whole of what they had loſt, which was a Benefit to themſelves, and to their Creditors in other parts of *India* and in *Europe.* Beſides, as many of them had acquired their Fortunes by their Induſtry, and had ſpent almoſt their whole Lives in this Climate, it was not only a Piece of Juſtice to recover for them what they had loſt, but a Point of true Policy to prevent the Terror of their Fate from having a miſchievous Operation

tion in succeeding Times, which otherwise it might have had; and this too in many Respects. The extending this Restitution to the *Jentoows* and *Armenians*, was not only a very exemplary but a very generous Act of Benevolence, founded in Principle. At the same time that it attached the particular Persons who were relieved, it raised the Reputation of the Company. It revived the Spirits of those useful Inhabitants, and gave a new Spring to their Activity and Industry, which were not only salutary Consequences at the Time, but will be found more so in their Effects, and facilitate the Execution of those Designs, that will be hereafter mentioned. This Tenderness for other Nations, this laudable Desire that they should share in the Prosperity, who had been hurt by the Adversity of the *English*, might be set in a far stronger Light, if placed in Comparison with the Conduct of others, without stirring out of *India*; but as that would be invidious, it is better omitted.

This stupendious Revolution may be also considered as equally glorious and advantageous to the *British* Nation. We may be allowed to ſay, becauſe the Fact cannot be diſputed, that it is a ſignal Proof of the Utility of Maritime Empire. As Commerce carries the Subjects of *Britain* every where, *Britiſh* Subjects every where experience *Britiſh* Protection: There are no Limits to our Naval Power, but thoſe by which the Creator has confined the Globe. The *Eaſt India* Company was ſaved, and her Affairs reſtored, by the Attention and Arms of that Government by which ſhe was erected. Many of thoſe, who would have totally loſt the Fruits of long Labour and various Hardſhips, and who muſt have been Beggars if ſubject to any other Power, are again eaſy in their Fortunes, and ſome of them have already tranſported their Effects to their native Country; the proper Return for the Aſſiſtance they derived from her maternal Affection; and as theſe Events have diſtinguiſhed the preſent Age and the preſent Adminiſtration, ſo their Effects will probably be felt in ſucceeding Times. The Company, by an Acceſſion of Territory, has an Opportunity of making an ample Settlement; which, under proper Management, may be not only extremely ſerviceable to her, but alſo to the

Nation;

Nation; and having a Revenue from these Lands, the Mint at *Calcutta*, and the Lease of the Salt-petre at *Patna*, which amounts in the whole to One hundred thousand Pounds a Year, there is a Provision against future Dangers upon the Spot, and without farther Expence. These Benefits have clearly arisen from that Revolution, of which we have given an Account, and are due to those who conducted it. May the future Emoluments do the like Honour to those who shall hereafter have the Care of the Company's and the Nation's Concerns in the *Indies*!

F I N I S.